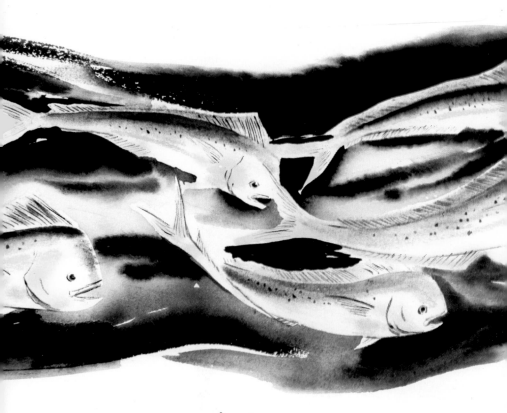

Al Pflueger's

Fisherman's
HANDBOOK

Text by Al Pflueger Jr.
Designed and illustrated by Russ Smiley

A few words...
right from the fishes mouth!

There are fish experts and there are fishing experts, but seldom do you find both in the same package. Al Pflueger is one of those rare combinations.

As an angler, Al undoubtedly has taken home more trophies and awards than any other fisherman, and also has posted more club, tournament and world records — with all classes of tackle. He was the youngest member ever to win the rank of Master Angler in the prestigious Rod and Reel Club of Miami Beach.

But more revealing than even his awe-inspiring array of accomplishments is the regard in which he is held by fellow sport fishermen. In a South Florida area where true fishing experts are plentiful, and where competition for both trophies and recognition is a way of life, Al Pflueger is respected as top hand.

Long before he became a dedicated angler, however, Al was a student of fish. He literally grew up among many thousands of specimens from all over the world in the renowned Pflueger Marine Taxidermy plant, founded by his late father, Al Pflueger Sr. And from the elder Pflueger, young Al inherited a burning interest in fishes from a naturalist's standpoint as well as an angler's.

In addition to working with the specimens that poured into the plant while Al learned every phase of the taxidermy business from skinning to managing, there were countless hours of SCUBA diving and observing fish in their natural habitat; of experimental fishing for rare deep-sea varieties; of maintaining an elaborate salt-water aquarium and collecting for it; and, of course, the long study of game fishes and their response to angling methods.

Al has been the subject of many magazine stories and has appeared several times on network television.

Certainly, nobody is better qualified to write a book on the fish and the fishing of southern waters, or could do it with more authority.

There's no better proof of this than this book itself. Once you look it over, you're bound to agree.

Vic Dunaway

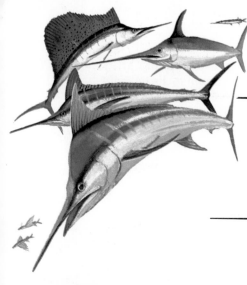

CON

Ocean and Gulfstream
page 6 thru 19

Bottom Fishing
Ocean and Reef
page 20 thru 37

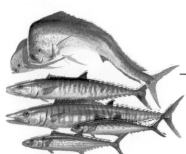

Fishing Inshore
Waters
page 38 thru 49

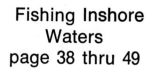

Fresh Water
Gamefish
page 50 thru 57

Sharks and Rays
page 58 thru 63

N T S

Marine Tropicals
page 64 thru 67

Deep Water Fishing
page 68 thru 69

Fish Identification
Photos
page 70 thru 91

Cross Index
page 92 thru 94

Ocean and Gulfstream

The deep sea. Blue Water. The Gulf Stream. Hunting grounds for the biggest game fish of all, and the most spectacular. Many people think of all big-game fishing in South Atlantic waters as Gulf Stream fishing, and though the Gulf Stream does certainly draw the greatest number of offshore sportsmen because of its proximity to established fishing ports, it is not the *only* great deep-sea territory, by any means.

Trophy seekers also hunt the Gulf of Mexico, the Caribbean and many areas of the Atlantic far removed from that famous offshore river known as the Gulf Stream. A handy term with which to categorize all angling of this sort is "blue-water fishing" — referring to the deep ocean, where great depth erases the greens and aquamarines that are the predominant colors of shallower water near shore.

Acknowledged stars of the blue-water angling world are the billfishes, from the great blue marlin and broadbill swordfish to the smaller but equally spectacular white marlin and sailfish, and the rare spearfish. However, the deep blue harbors many other sensational gamesters as well. Some of them, such as the giant bluefin tuna and the yellowfin or Allison tuna, rate right along with the billfishes in the big-game hierarchy. Others, including wahoo, king mackerel, many varieties of smaller tuna, the dazzling dolphin and great barracuda offer unforgettable sport and excitement to anglers willing to scale their tackle accordingly.

At one time, almost all blue-water fishing was surface trolling. This still is the predominant system everywhere, but in my years of fishing the deep blue, I've seen many other productive and exciting styles of offshore fishing develop — with all kinds of tackle — and I've been lucky enough to try most of them and perhaps even contribute a few new techniques of my own. In the following paragraphs we'll examine a number of ways to fish blue water, but with emphasis, of course, on surface trolling, because that still is the ticket for most anglers to get the most variety.

All the popular ocean fish, from giant marlin to small bonito, are regularly taken by skipping a rigged bait (or perhaps a specialized artificial lure) on the surface. Many different baits are used, the most popular being either small balao (ballyhoo) or small mullet. Strip baits, cut and fashioned from fillets of bonito or other fish, also rate high on my own list, and in the esteem of many professional captains.

Balao, finger mullet and strip baits are in the class often referred to as "sailfish baits"; that is, they are most attractive to fish in the sailfish class and smaller. For marlin and other big-game species, the chosen baits are larger — principally big mullet or whole mackerel. Whole bonefish, small barracuda and some other varieties are often chosen as marlin baits.

The rule of "big bait, big fish" is a standard one worth following, but, on the other hand, I have often seen blue marlin go for a tiny balao bait, or a relatively small sailfish or dolphin jump all over a large rigged mackerel. You never know, and so I like to have a variety of baits skipping behind the boat.

Tackle for offshore fishing has traditionally been scaled to several line-test classes set up by the International Game Fish Association. World records are kept by the IGFA in each of those line tests, which are 12, 20, 30, 50, 80 and 130. Only a short time ago, the IGFA added a 6-pound line class, but this certainly is too light to consider ever for blue water fishing, except in the hands of experienced anglers and even then in carefully chosen situations.

I feel the best all-around line class for blue-water fishing is 30-pound. Such gear affords fine sport with comparatively small fish, such as school dolphin and small tuna, and is entirely suitable for handling most anything you *normally* encounter in a day's offshore trolling, including sailfish and white marlin. Of course, you're in trouble if a big blue marlin or outsize Allison tuna decides to hit. It can happen, but it's rare.

Now, if you are deliberately seeking blue marlin you should choose at least 50-pound line, and better 80-pound if you're not too experienced or have hopes of getting a really giant fish.

The huge bluefin tuna which migrate in the western Bahamas and some other areas in the spring require 130-pound line — that and a strong back!

What about lines lighter than 30-pound-test? Well, you might go to 20 or 12 for added challenge after you get a few good fish on the 30-pound, or you might use light line for more selective fishing, such as for school dolphin or king mackerel.

Since the main goal of the blue-water troller is a billfish, outriggers are extremely helpful. These long poles angling from either side of the boat serve several useful purposes and were originally developed specifically for billfishing. The line is clipped to a pin on the outrigger cord, and the pin then is hoisted to the top of the 'rigger. Because the two outriggers spread the trolling lines far apart, there is room for another line or two to be trolled "flat" (directly from rod to water without an outrigger).

While the outrigger does allow you to troll more lines, and consequently different baits, its primary purpose is to provide an automatic "drop-back", which is the key to successful billfishing.

Seldom does a sailfish or marlin inhale a bait deeply enough on the strike so that you can hook him at once. It is vital that you drop back — give slack line as soon as he hits. With an outrigger, the drop-back is started for you automatically. With a flat-line, you must put your reel into free-spool and let the line flow back with only enough pressure from your thumb to prevent a backlash. For that matter, the automatic drop-back of the outrigger usually isn't enough, so as soon as the line leaves the pin you should free-spool and get ready to feed additional line.

Unfortunately, there is no rule of thumb that will tell you how long or how far to drop back. I've heard some people say "count 10 and then strike". I wish it were that simple. A 10-count many times is too long. Other times it's too short.

What you should try to do is be ready to throw the reel into gear and strike hard as soon as you feel the fish really taking out line with some speed. I admit this is difficult for a beginner because the boat is still moving forward and line will be leaving the reel even if the fish has dropped the bait. But if that reel spool is turning *fast* under your thumb, hit him!

Even the experts don't connect all the time. But if you miss on that first strike, here's a trick that will generally give you a second, or even a third chance. When you strike and feel nothing there, immediately raise your rodtip and crank the reel as fast as you can to bring the bait back to the top of the water and start it skipping once more. The fish will very often think his meal is getting away, and will chase and snare it once more. As soon as you see him coming, you must throw the reel into free-spool and hold the line tight with your thumb. Then, when he takes again, you ease thumb pressure and let him have line — but remember to maintain a little pressure to avoid that tragic backlash!

At this point something should be said about the individual billfishes. Sailfish are the most common and average about 30 to 60 pounds in weight. Believe it or not, sailfish as small as four or five pounds fall to offshore trollers using standard tackle and baits, and if you're lucky enough to get one of the little fellows it makes a beautiful trophy and discussion piece. Now with luck on

KING MACKEREL
Scomberomorus cavalla

Occurs in the North Atlantic, south to Brazil. Their food consists primarily of small fish and squid. Reaches a length of about 5 feet and a weight of 85 to 100 pounds.

WAHOO
Acanthocybium solanderi

A large pelagic species found in tropical Atlantic to North Carolina where it is not uncommon. Known to spawn in Florida straits. Reaches a length of over 6 feet and a weight of up to 150 pounds.

SPANISH MACKEREL
Scomberomorus maculatus

Occurs from South America to Maine. Very plentiful from North Carolina to the Gulf of Mexico. Feeds primarily on small fish, shrimp and squid. Reaches a weight of 10 to 15 pounds.

CERO
Scomberomorous regalis

Found from South America to Chesapeake Bay. More abundant in the Carolinas to the Florida Keys. Feeds primarily on small fish, squid and shrimp. Reaches a length of 4 feet and a weight of 20 pounds.

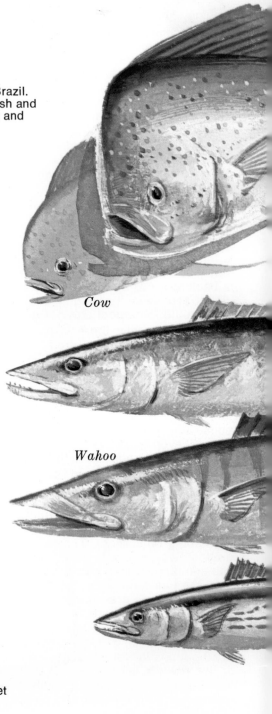

Cow

Wahoo

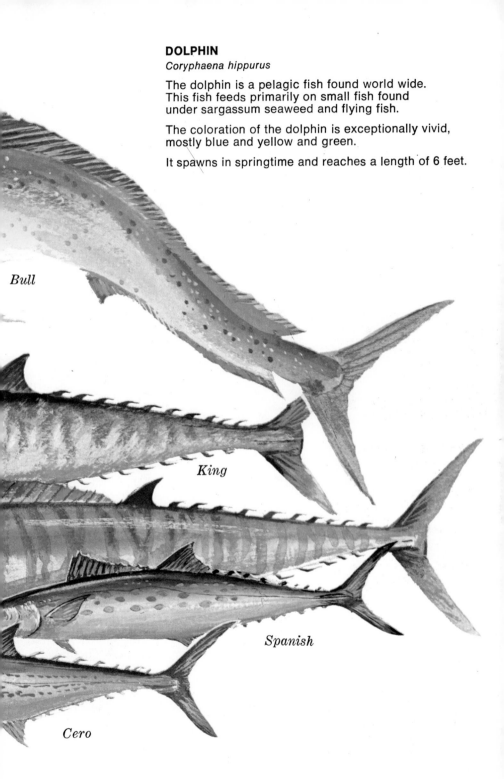

DOLPHIN
Coryphaena hippurus

The dolphin is a pelagic fish found world wide.
This fish feeds primarily on small fish found
under sargassum seaweed and flying fish.

The coloration of the dolphin is exceptionally vivid,
mostly blue and yellow and green.

It spawns in springtime and reaches a length of 6 feet.

Bull

King

Spanish

Cero

the other end of the scale, you can get a sail much heavier than average — maybe 80 or 90 pounds, and very rarely 100 or more.

White marlin aren't much larger than sailfish, on the average, yet they are the special pets of many blue-water fishermen because of their acrobatics, strength and beauty. Whites also give you a better shot at a 100-pound fish, since they are neither too common nor too rare at that weight. The maximum seems to be about 160 pounds, although there may be bigger ones in the sea.

The blue marlin is the Atlantic's premier billfish trophy ,and so varied in size that it is impractical even to state an "average".

However, I have seen hundreds of blues, and I suppose the majority of them have weighed between 125 and 400 pounds. There is no doubt the blue marlin can exceed 1000 pounds, even though the largest yet caught by a sports fisherman in Atlantic waters was 845 pounds. Blue marlin jump, often in spectacular fashion, but they are not as aerial-minded as their smaller relatives. Even on a pound-for-pound basis, however, they seem much more powerful than sailfish or white marlin and are rugged foes on any tackle; they remain one of the great big-game trophies of the world.

Two other varieties of billfish can be found in South Atlantic waters but both are so rare that anglers do not fish for them specifically. One is the great broadbill swordfish, the other the beautiful spearfish. One of the delights of offshore fishing is the ever present element of surprise — and no more welcome surprise could greet any angler than to connect with either one.

As to other blue-water game fish, a special favorite of off-shore fishermen is the dolphin. Dolphin are among the most beautiful of all fish, and marvelous table fare. But their game qualities, naturally, are what appeal to the angler. They often school heavily, and when a school is found, fantastic action can come your way in short order.

If you manage to work up a school of dolphin by surface trolling, then break out your casting tackle and have a ball. Once you hook one dolphin from a school, the others usually hang around so that you can see them and cast to them.

The most important tip I can give for dolphin fishing is never to boat a hooked fish until someone else in your party has another on the end of the line. A fresh school of dolphin is generally excited and all members are anxious to hit. In this state they will take artificial lures readily. Though they hit plugs, it's best to use single-hook lures, such as spoons or jigs because you'll have less trouble getting a boated fish off the hook. Toss your jigs either with spinning tackle or plug-casting gear. Although I enjoy both types of tackle, my favorite for this sort of dolphin fishing is the fly rod, because here is one of the most rewarding opportunities for the salt water fly caster — plenty of fish, close at hand, hungry and willing to hit at the surface. I like either white or yellow streamer flies, or large popping bugs in this situation.

There are other ways to keep a school of dolphin around your boat. First, toss out bits of chum, which can be pieces of

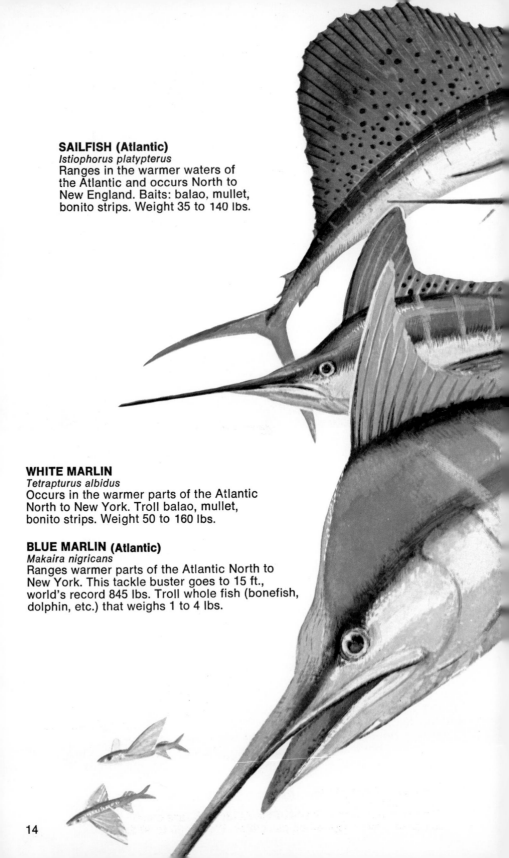

SAILFISH (Atlantic)
Istiophorus platypterus
Ranges in the warmer waters of
the Atlantic and occurs North to
New England. Baits: balao, mullet,
bonito strips. Weight 35 to 140 lbs.

WHITE MARLIN
Tetrapturus albidus
Occurs in the warmer parts of the Atlantic
North to New York. Troll balao, mullet,
bonito strips. Weight 50 to 160 lbs.

BLUE MARLIN (Atlantic)
Makaira nigricans
Ranges warmer parts of the Atlantic North to
New York. This tackle buster goes to 15 ft.,
world's record 845 lbs. Troll whole fish (bonefish,
dolphin, etc.) that weighs 1 to 4 lbs.

SWORDFISH
Xiphias gladius
Found in warm deep seas
North to Massachusetts.
Average 300 lbs. and run to 1200 lbs.

LONGBILL SPEARFISH
Tetrapturus pfluegeri
Ranges in the warmer parts of the Atlantic. A rare catch,
use same baits and method as sailfish. Weight 30 to 80 lbs.

15

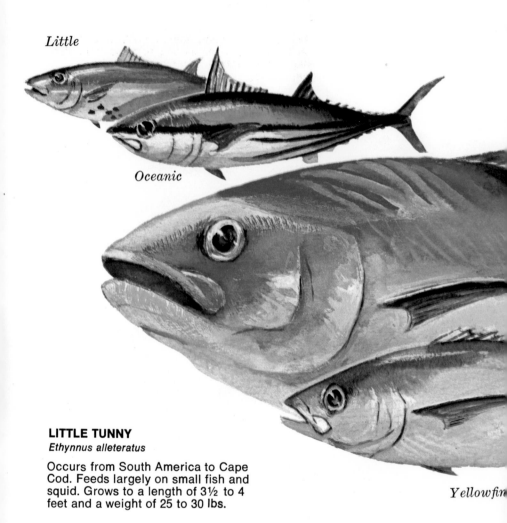

Little

Oceanic

Yellowfin

LITTLE TUNNY
Ethynnus alleteratus

Occurs from South America to Cape Cod. Feeds largely on small fish and squid. Grows to a length of 3½ to 4 feet and a weight of 25 to 30 lbs.

OCEANIC BONITO (Skipjack Tuna)
Euthynnus pelamis

A pelagic species found north to Cape Cod. Reaches a length of about 3 feet and a weight of about 25 to 30 lbs.

BLUEFIN TUNA
Thunnus thynnus

This tuna is the largest of the tunas. Found north to Nova Scotia. Feeds primarily on all small fish, mackerel and squid. Reaches a length of 11 feet and commercially caught up to 1100 lbs.

YELLOWFIN TUNA
Thunnus albacares

This species is found both in the Atlantic and Pacific. Feeds primarily on squid and small fish. Reaches a length of 7 feet and a weight of over 300 lbs.

ATLANTIC FLYINGFISH
Cypselurus heterurus

Found primarily in the warmer parts of the Atlantic and as far north as Nova Scotia. Reaches a length of 16 inches.

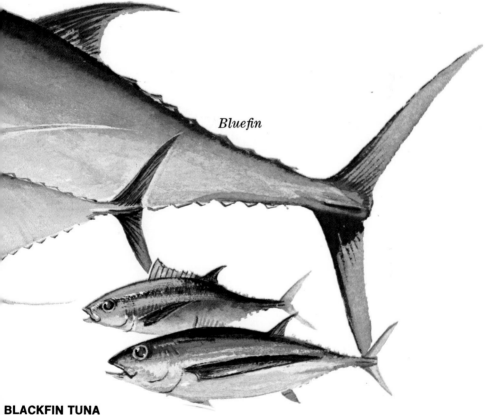

Bluefin

BLACKFIN TUNA
Thunnus atlanticus

Found as far north as Nova Scotia. Reaches a length of 4 feet and a weight of 40 lbs.

ALBACORE
Thunnus alalunga

Found in the Atlantic and Pacific. This fish is rare in Florida but is found as far north as Nova Scotia.

cut fish, pre-ground chum or even canned cat food. Also, commotion at the surface keeps their attention. If the school shows signs of fading, try swishing the surface hard with your rod, or rev your idling engine a little.

The really big dolphin are mostly solitary fish (or in pairs, one bull and one female) and are taken by trolling. But if casting into a school, be alert for the ever-present possibility that one or more big fish may join the act.

Dolphin are famous for their habit of sticking around floating weedlines or floating objects of any kind in the water. So investigate these whenever you see them.

Other types of schooling fish you may encounter are various species of small tuna, including the common bonito, oceanic bonito and blackfin tuna. Normally you'll spot these as they crash bait and churn up the surface. Try to troll around the edges of the disturbance, because running straight through the school invariably puts them down. Though not so easy as casting to dolphin, you can also cast into tuna schools, if you care to, by making a cautious approach.

King mackerel school thick in certain areas at certain times of the year. Since this is a migratory pattern you must get local information as to when king mackerel (also called kingfish) are schooling in local waters.

Though surface trolling will get kingfish, never is it apt to be so productive as underwater trolling, or drifting, or some other style of deep fishing.

I mentioned other systems of blue-water angling which are relatively new — at least new by means of popular acceptance if not actual age. One is drifting in blue water, rather than trolling. This style may be especially good for the private small boatman, because he can use either live bait, such as pilchard, blue runner, mullet or pinfish, and have a fine chance of catching all the species available to the trolling charter boat. Try keeping one live bait at the surface and another down pretty deep. And when you hook your sailfish, you never can tell if it will be on the surface or deep bait.

Kite fishing is a rather specialized drifting system in which a stout kite is flown downwind, carrying your fishing line in much the same fashion as an outrigger. On the end of your line is a frisky live bait, which can be kept at the surface or lowered below as you wish. With a kite out, you can deep-fish simultaneously on the other side of the boat.

Deep-trolling, using "downriggers", is also gaining much new acceptance. The downrigger is actually a sort of underwater outrigger — a separate and heavily weighted line to which your fishing line is attached by means of an outrigger-type pin. All types of open-ocean fish spend more of their time down deep than at the surface, and downrigger fishing is the most practical style of angling yet devised for trolling far below the surface.

Bottom Fishing
Ocean and Reef

A unique feature of tropical saltwater fishing is the coral reef — home to an infinite variety of fish, large and small, drab and unbelievably beautiful. The great majority of reef fish — discounting the tiny colorful species which are of interest only to aquarium fanciers — are good prospects for hook-and-line.

Now, of course, the hierarchy of bottom-fishing species is made up of those two famous families, the snappers and the groupers. Both groups contain many, many members of greatly varying size. Naturally, the larger snapper and grouper are the hoped-for prizes, although a bottom fisherman is always happy with some of the smaller fellows as well.

In the grouper family, the weight awards go to jewfish or giant sea bass, which can weigh 500 pounds or more. Almost as large as the Warsaw grouper, commonly weighing 100 pounds. The black grouper occasionally reaches 100 or more pounds, and in any size is perhaps the top favorite of grouper fishermen in general. Other favorite groupers are the red and Nassau. And those small groupers referred to as red hind and rock hind, weigh only a couple of pounds on the average, but are fun to catch and excellent eating.

There are many other groupers which the average angler seldom sees — deep water types, mostly. The spectacularly marked tiger grouper is common in some tropical reef areas, rare in others.

Among the snappers, the best known is the red snapper. This one is common in the deep waters of the open Gulf of Mexico and the Atlantic, seldom venturing into the shallower reef areas. In other words, red snapper are not often caught except on deliberate snapper trips by party or charter boat pretty far offshore. The most common large snapper of the tropical reefs is the mutton. Others in good supply are mangrove snapper (usually referred to as grey snapper when caught in the reefs), and schoolmaster snapper.

Giant among snappers is the cubera, which is common at 20 pounds and can easily weigh 100 or more. In South Florida, as well as most of the Bahamas and Caribbean Islands, the cubera is almost entirely a deep-water fish, spending most of its time near deep ledges, wrecks and reefs. In the Florida Keys, not many are taken except during spawning time in mid-summer when they come into about 120 feet of water just off the reef edges. Strangely, the cubera is a common resident of shallow inshore water on the east coast of Mexico and Central America, even roaming throughout coastal rivers.

Other types of "fishable" snapper include the dog snapper, a large fellow which is not so rare as the cubera nor so common as the mutton in Florida, and the small but very tasty lane snapper.

As with groupers, there are certain species of snapper which inhabit water so deep as to be beyond the reach of all but the most specialized fishing methods.

Just to add a bit of confusion, there is one favorite reef fish — the yellowtail — which doesn't wear the name "snapper", even though it is a member in good standing of the family. And another favorite reef fish, the hog snapper, isn't really a snapper at all, but a member of the wrasse family. It is more accurately called hog fish.

The major reefs of southern Florida and the Keys lie between the shoreline and deep blue water, their outlines being easily visible from the surface during clear water conditions. Such reefs also exist throughout the Bahamas and Caribbean, and at the edge of blue water along many stretches of the tropical American mainland.

In both the Atlantic and Gulf, north of Florida's southern sector, productive reefs are mostly well offshore, not visible from the surface, and not easy to find. For that matter, even in tropical waters where shallow reefs are common, there are additional reefs out in blue water — much deeper. Since the deeper, hidden reefs generally afford the best fishing for bigger fish, a good fathometer is a worthwhile investment for the ambitious bottom fishermen. Almost all charter and party boats have them.

With patience and luck, you can drift about and hit good bottom fishing over deep water. But, in my opinion, a good fathometer — one that records the bottom on a chart — is the most valuable piece of equipment an angler can invest in for reef or offshore angling.

For the bottom fisherman, an old angling saying applies most emphatically: "Big baits, big fish." It's true that you can take a good one occasionally on a small bait, but usually the little fellows will get a tiny bait first.

So if you have visions of big grouper or snapper, use large baits — a mullet head, or half a mullet, or perhaps a whole dead fish of smaller dimensions. Live bait is very effective in landing husky snapper and grouper. And if you don't have a supply with you, you could use a small hook and bait to catch your own, on the spot. A yellowtail is one of the best baits for large grouper. You could also use blue runner, grunts, smaller snapper, or anything else you manage to catch.

Fish the big baits, either live or dead, with patience if you want the 'lunkers'. But if you want action on smaller fish too, there's nothing wrong with tossing out, say, a mullet head on a big outfit and setting the rod in a holder while you fish with smaller baits for lesser fish.

Live shrimp, cut mullet, squid, dead shrimp, and live or dead pilchards make fine baits for yellowtail and grey snapper, which, among all the smaller reef species are by far the most-sought. Both varieties usually hit better if you manage to get an unweighted bait down fairly deep. If you must use a sinker, put on the smallest one that will do the job.

Russ Smiley

LANE SNAPPER
Lutianus synagris
Ranges from Brazil to Florida and the Gulf.
Caught around inner reefs. Best bait is
crustaceans, cut bait. Average weight ¾ to 2 lbs.

GREY SNAPPER
Lutianus griseus
Found from the West Indies to Maine. Occurs
in shallow water commonly in the Florida Keys
and Gulf. Fish around mangrove roots bridges,
docks, inner and outer reefs. Weight from 1 to 14 lbs.

SCHOOLMASTER (Snapper)
Lutianus apodus
Known from Brazil to Florida, straggling
northward to Carolinas. Usually caught when
fishing for other bottom fish. Weights 1 to 10 lbs.

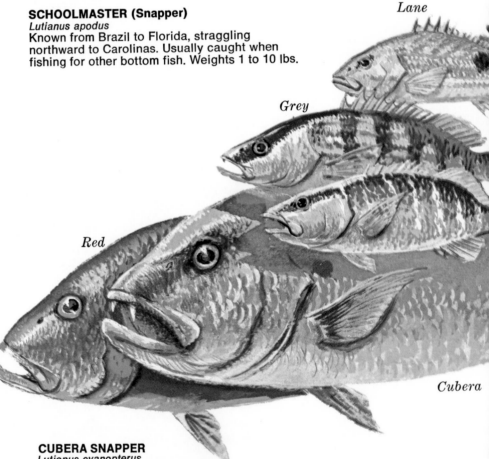

Lane

Grey

Red

Cubera

CUBERA SNAPPER
Lutjonus cyanopterus
Found in the Atlantic and Pacific
Caught bottom fishing, usually in
deep water. Average 25 to 150 lbs.

RED SNAPPER
Lutianus campechanus
Gulf of Mexico North to Carolina.
This fish is mainly caught in water
100 ft. or more. Caught bottom fishing
with cut bait. Weight to 50 lbs.

MUTTON SNAPPER
Lutjanus analis
Found from Brazil to Florida and northward
to Maine. Caught best still fishing
or slow deep trolling. Weight 4 to 30 lbs.

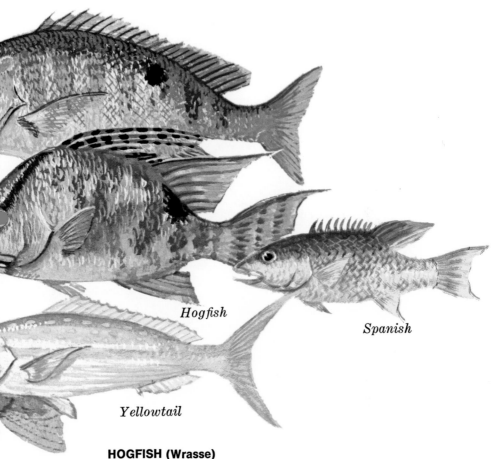

Hogfish

Spanish

Yellowtail

HOGFISH (Wrasse)
Lachnolaimus maximus
Found from West Indies North to Carolina. Caught on
inner and outer reefs. Feed on Crustacean. Weight 4 to 30 lbs.

YELLOWTAIL SNAPPER
Ocyurus chrysurus
Ranges from Brazil to Gulf of Mexico northward
to Carolina. Caught mainly over reefs. Still
fish with live shrimp, cut bait. Chum to
start them feeding. Weight 1 to 10 lbs.

SPANISH HOGFISH (Wrasse)
Bodianus rufus
A West Indies species reaching
northward to North Carolina.
Usually caught when fishing for
other bottom fish. Average ½ to 3 lbs.

BLACK MARGATE
Arisotremus surinamensis

West Indies north to the Florida
Straits. Feeds primarily on
crustaceans and small fish.
Reaches length of 36″.

BLUE STRIPED GRUNT
Haemulon sciurus

West Indies north to Florida.
Reaches length of 18″.

SPANISH GRUNT
Haemulon macrostomum

West Indies to Florida.
Not a common species.
Reaches 14″.

SAUCEREYE PORGY
Calamus calamus

Found from the West Indies to Florida. Feeds
primarily on crustaceans. Reaches length of 20″.

Porgy

Black Margate

Bluestriped

Spanish

Margate

French

FRENCH GRUNT
Haemulon flavolineatum

West Indies to Florida. Not commonly
caught. Reaches 12″.

MARGATE
Haemulon album

West Indies to Florida. Largest
of the grunts, reaches length
of 36″.

Squirrel

SQUIRREL FISH
Holocentrus ascensionis

Found from Brazil to Florida.
Reaches 24″, but rarely
caught over 12″.

Spade

ATLANTIC SPADEFISH
Chaetodipterus faber

West Indies to Cape Cod. Feeds
chiefly on invertebrates. Reaches 36″.

Orange

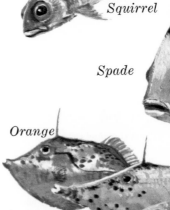

ORANGE FILEFISH
Aluterus schoepfii

Gulf Coast to Maine. Feeds primarily
on marine growths. Reaches 24″.

Scrawled

Cow

SCRAWLED FILEFISH
Aluterus scriptus

Found from West Indies to Maine.
Reaches 36″.

Trunkfish

COWFISH
Lactophrys quadricorn

Brazil to Maine.
Reaches 15″.

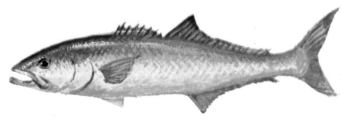

BLUEFISH
Pomatomus saltatrix

Atlantic and Indian Oceans.
Reaches 30 pounds.

TRUNKFISH
Lactophrys trigonus

Common in Florida, ranges to
Mass. Reaches 15".

BERMUDA CHUB
Kyphosus sectatrix

West Indies to Cape Cod.
Omnivorous in feeding.
Reaches 36".

QUEEN TRIGGERFISH
Balistes vetula

Ranges from tropics to Mass.
Reaches 24".

BLACK TRIGGERFISH
Melichthys niger

Tropical in range.
Reaches a length of 18".

OCEAN TRIGGERFISH (Tally)
Canthidermis sulflamen

Not common north of Florida.
Reaches a length of 24".

GRAY TRIGGERFISH
Balistes capriscus

Tropical in range. Reaches 30"

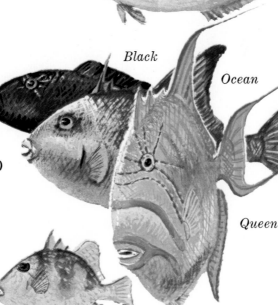

Chub

Black

Ocean

Queen

Grey

DOCTORFISH
Acanthurus chirurgus

Occurs West Indies, and Fla. Reaches
length of 12".

PORKFISH
Anisotremus virginicus

Ranges West Indies to Florida. Reaches 12".

SERGEANT-MAJOR
Abudefduf saxatilis

Ranges both coasts of tropical America.
Reaches a length of 8".

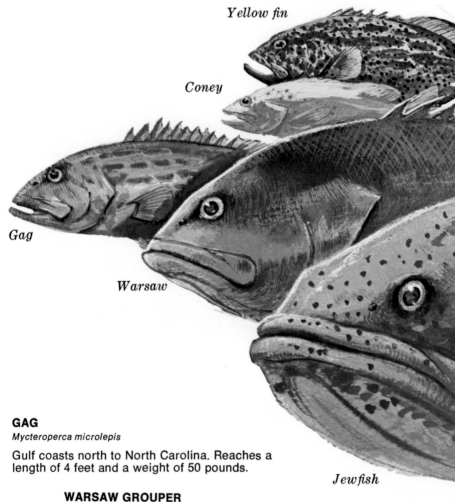

Yellow fin

Coney

Gag

Warsaw

Jewfish

GAG
Mycteroperca microlepis

Gulf coasts north to North Carolina. Reaches a length of 4 feet and a weight of 50 pounds.

WARSAW GROUPER
Epinephelus nigritus

Ranges from Brazil to South Carolina. Reaches a length of 7 feet and a weight of 700 pounds.

JEWFISH
Epinephelus itajara

Ranges from both coasts of the tropical America, north to Florida. Largest of the Sea Basses. Reaches a weight of over 1000 pounds and a length of 8 feet.

YELLOWFIN GROUPER
Mycteroperca venenosa

Ranges from West Indies north to
Florida. Reaches a weight of 30
pounds and a length of 3 feet.

GOLDEN CONEY
Epinephelus fulvus

West Indies to Florida. Feeds
primarily on crustaceans.
Reaches a length of 1 foot.

SICKLE-FIN GROUPER
Dermatolepis — inermis

Ranges East tropical coast of
America. Reaches a weight of 20
pounds and a length of 4 feet.

TIGER GROUPER
Mycteroperca tigris

Ranges from West Indies to Florida.
Reaches a length of 2 feet.

GRAYSBY
Epinephelus cruentatus

Ranges from Brazil to Florida. Reaches a length of 14″.

BLACK GROUPER
Mycteroperca bonaci

Ranges from West Indies to North Carolina. Reaches a
length of 5 feet and weight of 100 pounds.

NASSAU GROUPER
Epinephelus striatus

Ranges from Brazil to North Carolina. Reaches a length
of 4 feet and a weight of 50 pounds.

RED HIND
Epinephelus guttatus

Ranges from Brazil to South Carolina. Reaches a
length of about 24″.

MARBLED GROUPER
Dermatolepis inermis

Ranges from Brazil to Florida. Reaches a
length of 4 feet

ROCK HIND
Epinephelus adscensionis

Ranges from West Indies to North Carolina.
Reaches a length of 2 feet.

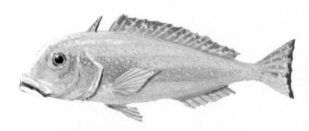

TILEFISH
Lopholatilus chamaleonticeps

Ranges from Florida to Maine.
Reaches a weight up to 50 pounds.

Graysby

Nassau

Red

Marbled

Rock

31

GREAT BARRACUDA
Sphyraena barracuda

Ranges from West Indies to South Carolina. Reaches a length of 7 feet and 100 pounds in weight.

AFRICAN POMPANO
Alectis crinitus

Ranges from both tropical coasts of America. Reaches a length of 4 feet and a weight of 50 pounds.

African

BAR JACK
Caranx ruber
Caught on reefs year around.
Average 2 lbs. and run to 10 lbs.

Bar

CREVALLE JACK
Caranx hippos

Ranges from West Indies to North Carolina. Feeds primarily on small fish. Reaches a length of 4 feet and a weight of 50 pounds.

Crevalle

GREATER AMBERJACK
Seriola dumerili

Ranges from both tropical coasts of America to North Carolina. Reaches a length of 7 feet and a weight of 150 pounds.

Amberjack

FLORIDA POMPANO
Trachinotus carolinus

Ranges from Gulf coast to Virginia. Reaches a length of 30 inches and a weight of 8 pounds.

Blue

BLUE RUNNER
Caranx crysos

Ranges from both tropical coasts of America to North Carolina. Reaches a length of 24 inches and a weight of 8 pounds.

Lookdown

PERMIT
Trachinotus falcatus

Ranges from the West Indies to Florida. Reaches a length of 4 feet and a weight of 80 pounds.

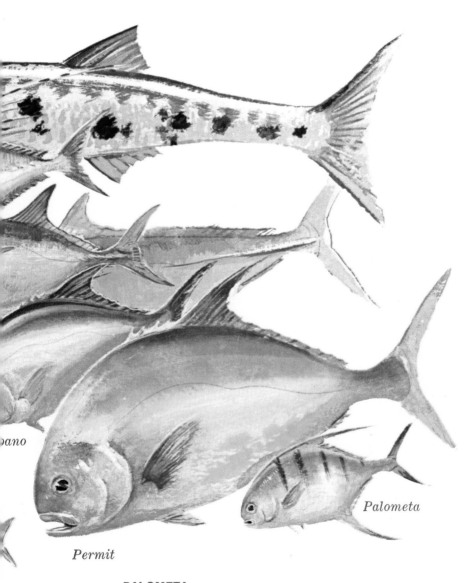

pano

Permit

Palometa

PALOMETA
Trachinotus goodei

Ranges from the West Indies to Florida. Reaches a length of 20 inches and a weight of 4 pounds.

LOOKDOWN
Selene vomer

Ranges from Brazil to North Carolina. Reaches a length of 16 inches and a weight of 4 pounds.

QUEEN ANGELFISH
Holacanthus ciliaris

A West Indies species ranging to Florida. Reaches a length of 2 feet.

FRENCH ANGELFISH
Pomacanthus paru

Occurs from the West Indies to Florida. Reaches a length of 16".

GRAY ANGELFISH
Pomacanthus arcuatus

Ranges from Brazil to North Carolina. Reaches a length of 24".

ROCK BEAUTY
Holocanthus tricolor

Ranges from the West Indies to Florida. Reaches a length of 1 foot.

BANDED BUTTERFLYFISH
Chaetodon striatus

Ranges from West Indies to Florida. Reaches a length of 7".

FOUREYE BUTTERFLYFISH
Chaetodon capistratus

West Indies to Florida. Reaches a length of 7".

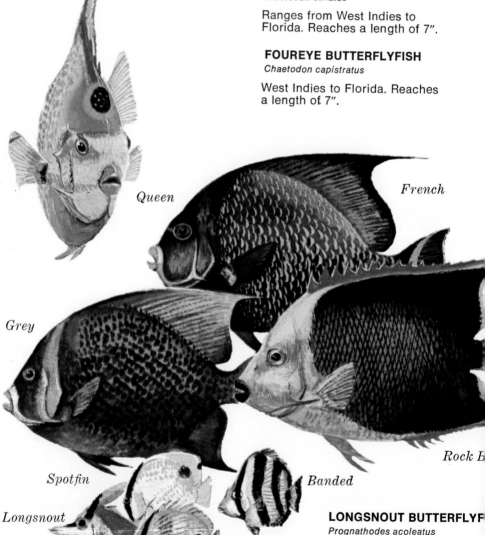

Queen

French

Grey

Rock B

Spotfin

Banded

Longsnout

LONGSNOUT BUTTERFLYF
Prognathodes acoleatus

West Indies to Florida. Reac a length of 7".

Foureye

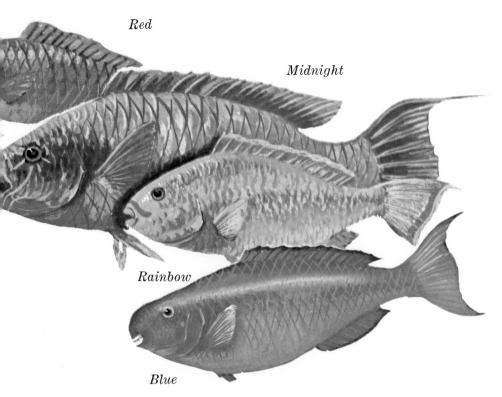

Red

Midnight

Rainbow

Blue

RED PARROTFISH

Nicholsina usta

Ranges from the West Indies to Florida. Reaches a length of 18″.

MIDNIGHT PARROTFISH

Scarus coelestinus

West Indies to Florida. Reaches 24″ and a weight of 5 lbs.

RAINBOW PARROTFISH

Scarus guacamaia

Occurs West Indies to Florida. The largest of the parrotfish, reaching 3½ feet and a weight of 35 lbs.

BLUE PARROTFISH

Scarus caeruleus

Occurs West Indies to North Carolina. Reaches 3 feet and a weight of 20 lbs.

POTFIN BUTTERFLYFISH

aetodon ocellatus

est Indies to North Carolina. eaches a length of 8″.

Chumming with ground fish always helps produce reef action. Particularly at night, but often in daylight, a good chum stream will raise yellowtail and grey snapper, and even grouper, up near the surface.

Heavy boat tackle is a necessity if you hope to haul up big bottom fish with any regularity while still-fishing. Spinning and plug tackle are fine for grey snapper and yellowtail and many of the varied reef fish you might get with small baits, such as triggerfish, porgy, margate, angel fish, pork fish and that table favorite — grunt.

You can troll the reefs effectively, too. Use a whole rigged balao, a strip, or a feather-and-strip combination with a keeled trolling sinker. Grouper and snapper willingly hit trolled baits, as do many non-bottom fish which lurk around the reefs, including amberjack, bar jack, barracuda, cero mackerel and king mackerel.

Although I have recommended heavy tackle for big fish on the reefs, there are several specialties practiced regularly by light-tackle fanciers. If you like you can use spinning, plug or even fly tackle for reef-area fishing. Naturally, you're going to lose some big grouper in the rocks, but you'll catch more, as your experience grows. Meanwhile you can take plenty of gamesters which don't usually 'hole up on you.'

One such specialty is deep-jigging. For this you use either spinning or plug tackle, but you use a rod considerably heavier than you would select for the same weights of line inshore. While club and tournament fishermen of South Florida stick to 10-pound-test line on spinning tackle, and 15-pound-test with plug tackle, don't be bashful about using 20-pound line on either type of gear. You certainly won't be overloaded!

Deep-jigging usually is practiced over the deeper reefs, in water from about 80 to 150 feet deep. The system can be used effectively in shallower water, but my experience has indicated that it is easier to land a big bottom fish on light tackle in deep water than in shallow. Also, most of the time you have better odds of hooking big ones in the deep.

With this method, you use a lead-head jig weighing, generally, from 2 to 3½ ounces. You let this sink to bottom, then bring it up with continuous and strong upward sweeps of the rod. You might get bottom fish, or any of the pelagic fish nearer surface. Even a lot of sailfish have been hooked by using this method, as well as such great game varieties as African pompano, blackfin tuna, an occasional wahoo, amberjack, barracuda, king mckerel and cobia, plus many others.

Another light tackle specialty is what we call "chugger fishing" in South Florida. You use spin or plug tackle, again with heavier-than-normal rods, and toss big popping plugs out over the reef, *retrieving them at a fast rate of speed* and as much noise as you can make. Apparently, all the commotion makes game fish think that a school of bait is being attacked. Fish come to the noise from pretty long distances. You can sometimes even raise snapper and grouper up from the bottom for 30 feet or more. The chugging plug attracts just about any kind of predatory fish, and some of the biggest cero mackerel are caught this way. Even some of the smaller types, such as yellowtail, will come up to hit it.

Of course, both deep jigging and chugger fishing can get pretty tiring. To avoid working so hard at deep jigging, you can put a strip of cut bait on your jig, and merely let it drift down deep, or else bring it up with much less speed and work than would be necessary with a bare jig. Again, club and tournament anglers can't combine a lure with bait in some of their competitive divisions, but the guy out for fun isn't hampered by rules.

Some types of reef fish, most notably the cobia, require specialized methods. Actually, the cobia isn't a reef dweller *per se,* but I include it in this category because it is neither strictly an inshore fish nor a blue-water type.

Most cobia are caught either around offshore channel markers, or over wrecks, or perhaps in company with other large sea creatures such as big rays. Though very moody at times, cobia can be caught either on live baits or on the popular reef lures like jigs and chugging plugs.

If ambitious fly fishing interests you, be sure to carry your outfit along when fishing the reefs or the outside. Probably you'll want to reserve the fly for the times you see fish working at the surface, or for casting to specific spots, such as for cobia around markers.

Here's a tip that has paid off for me with a lot of fine flyrod catches: when someone else is working a chugger, it may raise fish which follow the plug but refuse to hit it. Often such reluctant followers will take a fly tossed out to the surface. And you might also be ready with your flyrod when your buddy is bringing a hooked fish close to the boat, because other fish frequently follow a hooked one all the way in — sometimes the same kind of fish that's on the line, and sometimes an entirely different species.

And for another tip: some of the most exciting times I've ever had while fishing over the reefs have been provided by the "decoy system". Try it. Use a live blue runner or small jack as a decoy, letting him swim around and make as much surface noise as possible. But be sure to use the decoy on a stout boat rod or maybe a calcutta pole so you'll have some control over him. After all, the idea is to tease big fish to the side of your boat, but not let them have the bait. The idea is to get the prize excited and chasing the decoy, but to pull it away when he goes after it. By using this system, I have had amberjack and other game species literally boiling the water all around the boat, and wild enough to grab a fly or other lure as soon as it hits the water.

On the whole, for sheer variety, and for action on most anything from a mess of grunts to a huge grouper, you could hardly find a better fisherman's playground than the warm-water reefs.

Fishing Inshore Waters

Inshore fishing action comes in many packages and many settings — perhaps on a shallow, clear flat; perhaps from a pier or bridge or standing at the edge of the surf; perhaps in a rushing inlet or tidal river; maybe in a quiet cove or along a secluded shoreline, or drifting over grass beds, or casting to the edges of oyster bars. Also, inshore fishing might be anything from a heart-stopping struggle with a giant tarpon to lazy and relaxed angling for spotted sea trout.

There are more than enough possibilities for every angling taste, and most anglers have their particular favorites. My own favorite? I guess I'd have to say all of them, because I love to fish any way there is to fish. In the right season you'll certainly find me throwing big streamer flies at giant tarpon on the flats of the Florida Keys. But you're just as likely to see me sneaking

off after work to a quiet bayfront where ladyfish are supposed to be hitting.

Let's look individually at some of the many varieties of coastal fishing in southern waters.

Bonefish are considered by many as the king of light-tackle gamesters, combining power and incredible speed with a wariness that makes them a challenge to the most skillful angler. Even so, the bonefish maintains his title as "king" only because he is more numerous and accessible to more anglers than is the permit, a huge species of pompano which often shares the same water with bonefish.

Though bonefish can be caught by still-fishing on bottom in fairly deep water, the classic method is to stalk them on clear and shallow flats, searching through polarizing sunglasses while quide or companion poles a skiff. You can practice the same system while wading and, occasionally, while drifting.

By all means, the aspiring bonefisherman should begin his efforts with a professional guide. Excellent guides are available everywhere in established bonefish territory, which includes extreme South Florida, the Bahamas, Bermuda, all the islands of the Caribbean and tropical Atlantic, and the Atlantic shores of Central America. Permit can be found throughout the same range, and somewhat farther north than bonefish. They are never nearly so plentiful as bones, but can be more easily fished for in locations other than shallow flats.

Standard tackle for bonefishing is a light-to-medium spinning outfit, the reel spooled with at least 200 yards of 8 or 10-pound-test line. Heavier lines make casting difficult with the necessary light baits and lures.

Leading bait for bonefish is live shrimp. Dead ones often work well, and where shrimp is not available try small crabs or pieces of crab or pieces of conch.

Like bonefish, permit will accept live shrimp, particularly if you skitter it across the surface until you attract their attention and then allow it to settle. But the best permit bait of all is a small live crab.

As to artificial lures, small jigs are the ticket — one-eighth ounce, if you can cast that light weight efficiently, one-quarter ounce if you must. Heavier jigs will take bones but are difficult to work without hanging in extremely shallow water.

I doubt that any other salt water fish is so dear to the hearts of flycasters as the bonefish. They take flies readily — sometimes better than spinning lures. And on the shallowest "tailing" flats, a flyrod in the hands of an accomplished caster is the best medicine short of a live shrimp.

Small bucktail flies and shrimp imitations, tied on No. 2, 1 or 1/0 hook are most often used. Though color is not so important as many think, popular hues of flies are white, brown, brown-white, yellow-white and pink.

Permit take jigs pretty well, but of all the inshore fish that will take a fly, permit are undoubtedly the least avid fly-grabbers. Capturing a permit is one of the main ambitions of fly fishermen.

When you are fighting either bonefish or permit, a light drag is essential because of the incredibly long runs made by even a modest-size bone. Line disappears from the spool so rapidly that with a heavy drag, tension builds to the breaking point before you realize it. The drag should not be more than one-third of the line's test.

Also, that long run necessitates that you hold your rod high overhead. This helps keep more of the line out of the water — or at least high in the water — thus lessening the danger of cut-off as the line is dragged across coral or sea fans.

Bonefish being caught blindly in deep water usually is accidental. Permit, on the other hand, can be found regularly in certain deep-water situations — principally over known wrecks, but also over reefs and in some deeper inshore holes. In deep water, permit are less choosy about hitting artificials, but the best natural bait still is the small crab.

TARPON

Tarpon have been called the "big-game fish of inshore waters". This is quite an apt description, but an incomplete one, because tarpon come in so many sizes and settings that any angler, with any kind of tackle, can find great fun with them. And the fish is a truly spectacular prize, whether it weighs two pounds or 200 pounds. Tarpon range throughout the tropics and, unlike the bonefish, also inhabit temperate waters during warm seasons.

If seeking big tarpon, you should use heavy boat rods with star drag reels as standard equipment. Average line size is 40 or 50-pound test, although experienced folks frequently choose lighter line.

Baits vary widely. In channels and other deep areas, live bait is generally chosen, the most used ones being mullet or pinfish or live crab. Usually live baits are drifted or trolled very slowly, although they can also be fished from a bridge or anchored boat, usually with a float.

Along the Florida Gulf Coast, a lot of big tarpon are caught in shallow bays on dead baits which are fished on bottom. Again, either a half-mullet or a whole dead pinfish is the normal choice.

You can also get big tarpon by trolling with heavy tackle and huge spoons, or oversized plugs with extra-strength hooks designed specifically for such work. Large feathers, and even some of the offshore rigged baits, such as balao, are preferred in some areas of the Florida Keys.

Tarpon make excellent targets for fly plug and spin casters with artificial lures. Generally, casters seek the small to medium-size fish, but it is now an established practice to go after the giant specimens, too, on casting gear. This specialty is most highly developed around Islamorada in the Florida Keys, but is practiced to varying degrees wherever casters find big tarpon.

Tarpon are willing to strike almost any type of saltwater lure, but in their own good time. No fish is more stubborn. On those shallow Florida Keys flats, large streamer flies are the most productive lures — so productive that the popular spinning and casting lures down that way are merely weighted versions of the streamer.

Elsewhere, when casting blind or to rolling fish, plugs are usually the first and foremost lures — both surface models and underwater styles. A great favorite is the mirror-finish plug. Jigs get a lot of strikes from tarpon, and particularly in deep or running water.

Incidentally, I should point out that if you cast for big tarpon and have any choice in the matter whatever, throw your lures in as shallow water as possible. In deep water, big tarpon like to use depth and strength to battle light tackle. In the shallows, they have little choice but to jump and spend their energy more quickly. Even in shallow water, you'll probably be in for a long and tough fight, but your chances are a lot better than in deep water.

Anglers hook far more tarpon than they land, because the fish's bony mouth is darn good protection against a hook. My best advice for increasing your percentage of hookups, and for carrying the battle with a good fish to a successful conclusion includes four main points:

1. Strike *hard* several times whenever you get a hit from a tarpon. Strike as hard as your drag will stand.

2. Strike again for good measure whenever a tarpon completes a series of jumps and settles down underwater.

3. "Bow" to the fish on every jump — that is, quickly lean far forward, extending your rod out and down, to throw as much slack line as possible.

4. This is a simple and basic point, but one of the most important. Sharpen your hooks and see that they stay sharp!

SNOOK

Most people think of snook as a fish of the shorelines and mangrove roots — which is perfectly correct, but not a complete picture. Throughout its range, which includes the lower half of both Florida coasts, plus all of tropical America, snook are commonly found, not only along hidden shorelines, but also in bays and inlets, around piers and bridges, and even on reefs.

Moreover, in many places the snook is a leading customer of surf fishermen. Despite its widespread habitat, the snook is never an easy fish to take, and angling for the species is often highly specialized. Even if you happen to be a top snook fisherman in one particular situation, you must seek out as much advice as possible when you go snooking in a new environment, or under unfamiliar conditions.

Should you prefer natural bait, large live shrimp are generally dependable, as are many types of small baitfish. Among the latter, pinfish and finger mullet rate as the most popular, but you can also get snook with pilchards, or small blue runners or, for that matter, many different types of baitfish that inhabit the local waters.

When it comes to artificials, snook are every bit as democratic as the largemouth bass in that they have been taken on just about every imaginable lure. But it pays to have a good assortment of plugs, jigs and spoons at hand when you cast for snook, because their appetites and whims are highly changeable.

In the "classic" snook situation — casting to mangrove roots and other likely shoreline spots — darting surface plugs have long been the number one choice. And the same situation is an excellent one for the fly caster, using fairly large streamer or hair flies, preferably yellow, or a mixture of yellow with other colors.

Either along the shore, or in other shallow waters, some more good lure choices are mirror plugs, shallow-running swimming plugs, spoons and jigs. In deeper water, where snook are reluctant to romp at or near the surface, there's nothing better than a leadhead jig bounced slowly along the bottom.

Snook are great night feeders, and in some areas (the Florida East Coast, particularly) many more are taken after dark than in the daylight hours. Bridges and docks in snook country almost invariably afford some night-time action. For the boater who wants to work after dark, inlets and passes are attractive territory.

Any kind of casting tackle can be used effectively for snook fishing. Heavier gear is often called for when obstacles are close at hand, especially bridge pilings.

Russ Smiley

SNOOK
Centropomus undecimalis

Ranges from West Indies to Florida.
Reaches a length of 4 feet and a
weight of 50 pounds.

SPOTTED SEATROUT (Weakfish)
Cynoscion nebulosus

Ranges from Gulf coast to North Carolina. Reaches a length of 3 feet and weight of 16 pounds.

RED DRUM (Channel Bass)
Sciaenops ocellata

Ranges from Texas to Virginia. Reaches a length of 5 feet and a weight of 85 pounds.

DRUM
Pogonias cromis

Reaches a weight of 110 lbs.

BROAD FLOUNDER
Paralichthys squamilentus

Ranges from the Gulf coasts to Florida. Reaches a length of 24″.

COBIA
Rachycentron canadum

Common on our coast of Florida to Chesapeake Bay. Reaches a length of 6 feet and a weight of 100 pounds.

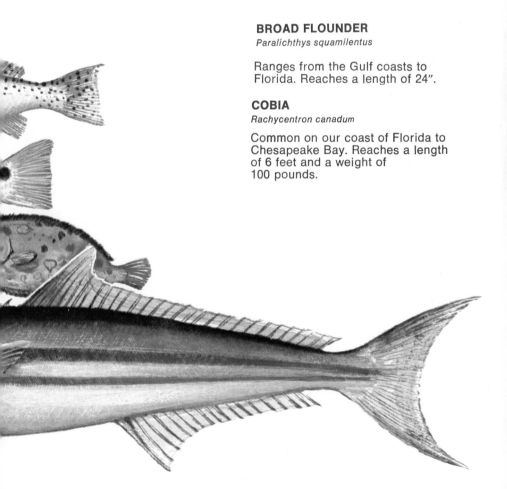

SHEEPSHEAD
Archosargus probatocephaius

Ranges from Texas to Cape Cod.
Reaches a length of 35 inches and
a weight of 20 pounds.

TRIPLETAIL
Lobotes surinamensis
Caught near shore, wrecks, rocky bott
Average 5 lbs. and run to 60 lbs.

FANTAIL MULLET
Mugil trichodon

Ranges from Brazil to Florida.
Reaches a length of 1 foot.

TARPON
Megalops atlantica

Ranges from Brazil to North
Carolina. Reaches a length of 8
feet and a weight of 350 pounds.

BONEFISH
Albula vulpes

Ranges in all warm seas, north to
Florida. Reaches a length of 36
inches and weight of 20 pounds.
Feeds primarily on crustaceans.

LADYFISH
Elops saurus

Ranges from all warm seas to
North Carolina. Reaches a length
of three feet.

WEAKFISH OR SEA TROUT

I'm sure the spotted seatrout must be by far the most popular inshore game fish of southern coastal waters. It's a favorite because it is often easier to come by than other game species, fights a showy battle, and makes a tasty dish as well.

A close relative, the common weakfish (also called grey trout) is not nearly so widely distributed in southern waters, but is important in certain scattered localities. There's another weakfish, called the silver or white trout, which is very common in most coastal waters of the Gulf of Mexico. The silver is usually taken in deep water, while the speckled or spotted trout is primarily a flats dweller. However, the speckled variety also will seek deeper water during extreme cold or hot spells.

The universal system for taking speckled trout during periods of normal water temperatures, is to drift over large beds of grass in coastal waters. You can use either spin or plug tackle with the simplest or rigs — merely a hook tied to the end of your line, and baited with either a live shrimp or a strip of cut mullet. You simply let this trail along as the boat drifts.

If artificials are preferred, you can drift as you cast mirror plugs, jigs or surface plugs. A great favorite is the jig with a plastic worm or grub tail.

When trout are not to be found on the grassy flats, look for them along channel edges, around oyster bars, or in deeper potholes of flats country. Along with the use of natural bait in such places, the popping cork is an excellent device, and is merely a large float with a cupped head, which you pop noisily with your rodtip from time to time in order to attract the fish.

Trout are often found in the surf, and may be taken from piers and bridges, both night and day. During cold snaps, they often roam far into rivers and creeks, seeking warmer water.

MACKEREL AND BLUEFISH

While mackerel and bluefish are not closely related species, southern anglers often think of them as a team, because in most southern areas they arrive and leave at approximately the same time of year on migratory schedules.

Also, both species frequently succumb to the same angling methods; however, bluefish are perhaps less fussy in their striking habits. Blues will even take dead baits fished on bottom, whereas mackerel seldom hit a dead bait unless it is given lifelike action by drift or current.

Trolling is a standard system for mackerel fishing, and will also take a lot of blues. Small silver spoons and white nylon jigs do good work in trolling, but it you're after mackerel, remember that a pretty fast trolling speed is necessary — at least five or six knots.

When casting for mackerel it is essential to move the lure very fast, usually as fast as you can crank the reel, and with a lot of rod-whip thrown in for good measure.

Bluefish hit plugs better than do mackerel, although you can get mackerel on surface lures and certain underwater plugs with a fast or fast-darting action. Bluefish love a noisy surface lure, but are equally willing to take jigs or spoons. Most piers and a lot of bridges afford good action on both mackerel and bluefish during the proper season.

Though I have been referring primarily to the Spanish mackerel, which is mainly a fish of the inshore waters and bays, anglers in sub-tropical waters also get a great shot at another species — the cero mackerel. Most ceros are caught along the outside reefs, and even occasionally in blue water, although they sometimes stray close to shore. There is really no difference at all in fishing methods for Spanish or cero mackerel.

The cero averages slightly larger in size than the Spanish, and grows *much* larger. A 10-pound Spanish mackerel is a rare catch, but quite a few ceros of that size fall to anglers each year. The largest cero I ever saw was a 20-pounder, caught in the western Bahamas.

OTHER INSHORE FAVORITES

So far I have touched on just a few of the best-known and best-liked inshore fish in southern waters. There are, of course, a great many others — some, perhaps, just as popular as those already mentioned.

Certainly the channel bass, or redfish, is worthy of mention, since it is widely distributed and willing to hit bottom baits, surface plugs, and most natural and artificial baits in between. The biggest channel bass — and they can weigh 50 pounds or more — are usually caught by surf fishermen along the Atlantic shore. Big "bull redfish" also fall to surf men working the barrier islands of the Gulf Coast.

But smaller redfish are the ones that please most anglers, since they are available inshore around oyster bars, shell flats and gentle beaches. Like the speckled trout, they wander into freshwater rivers when the weather turns cold.

Reds feed mostly on crustaceans; therefore, shrimp and crab baits are the leading offerings. In shallow water they willingly take surface plugs, and will strike underwater plugs and spoons as well. But the best "artificial" bait no doubt is a jig with a small piece of shrimp on the hook. This combines the advantages of both bait and lure. Redfish seem to have a better sense of smell than sight.

No matter whether you fish with lure or bait in southern inshore waters — and no matter what particular kinds of fish you may be *trying* to catch — chances always are better than even that you'll take several varieties.

Most common game fish of all are the high-jumping ladyfish and the rugged jacks. Both rank among the best of fighters, but aren't too popular with regular fishermen because they are *too* easy to get on the end of a line.

Fishing in coastal waters also produces mangrove snapper, gag grouper, small jewfish, sheepshead, croaker, common sea bass, flounder and sand perch and a host of small but tasty catches that include grunts, spot, pinfish, porgy and numerous others. In general, the fisherman who isn't choosy is almost sure to find action and fun.

Fresh Water Game Fish

Fresh Water
Game Fish

Everybody's game fish is the largemouth bass, which is found in every state, and which also has been introduced to several Caribbean islands and at least one Central American lake — Lake Yojoa in Honduras.

In Florida, however, the largemouth has found its happiest home of all. Climate and water temperature allow for a long breeding season and year-round feeding activity, all of which means the chance for a near-record bass, while at the same time assuring an abundant supply of fish in all sizes, to keep the angler happy as he searches for the lunker. Moreover, largemouths are pretty hardy. They make themselves at home in virtually every freshwater setting — tidal brackish rivers, ponds, lakes, creeks, major rivers, and man-made canals. Obviously, this opens the door to many different systems of bass fishing in many different places. A couple of my favorites are fishing in areas of heavy vegetation, such as are encountered in the Everglades and Lake Okeechobee, and fishing roadside spots, many of which are overlooked by the average angler.

Now, in South Florida particularly, there are numerous road-side canals that are justly famous and attract thousands of bass seekers. But I'm talking mostly about the not-so-obvious smaller canals, ditches and burrow pits which are scattered generously along both major highways and rural roads in every sector.

While traveling, I'm always on the lookout for such spots and it doesn't take too long to work over many of these with a flyrod popper, or a surface plug or an artificial worm. And some of my heaviest bass have come from this sort of "pothole" fishing.

In the Everglades Conservation areas of Dade, Broward and Palm Beach Counties in South Florida — and also around the marshy edges of Lake Okeechobee — I like to get right out in the areas of thick aquatic vegetation and cast weedless spoons.

Usually I retrieve the spoon fairly fast and keep it on top — skimming it right over the lily pads and grasses and reeds, while guiding its path to cross as many open pockets of water as pos-sible. But the strikes don't always come in the open pockets. Bass just as often bull their way through the thickest weeds to smack the spoon with a loud crash.

It goes without saying that you need pretty heavy line to handle a bass in such a situation. I'd advise a minimum of 15-pound-test, while 20 certainly isn't too heavy. A plug casting outfit is the logical choice, though spinning gear can be used.

In addition to weedless spoons, I often use surface plugs when I encounter enough open areas in the grass to permit such use. Also, I use plastic worms, either for fishing to selected spots or else to throw immediately to a fish which rises to the spoon but refuses to take it.

In most other bass-fishing situations where the water is open, or reasonably open, the plastic worms undoubtedly are the chief strike-producers. The trend lately has been to the big worms, from 8 to 12 inches in length, fitted with a weedless hook, or rigged to special work hooks which also allow a weedless setup.

But the old favorite six-inch plastic worm is still a great bass-fooler, and especially good when you can allow it to drift naturally with the current. Flyrod fishermen rely mostly on floating bass plugs, but more and more of them are finding that a good-sized streamer fly will produce bass when the poppers just don't cut it.

Overall, there are plenty of bass-fishing opportunities for any kind of tackle you might care to use. Ultra-light and light spinning gear are great fun in open areas, and ideal for tossing several of the most consistently productive lures, such as the light balsa wood plugs, little spinners of various sorts, and the smaller artificial worms.

If you like to stress surface fishing, I'd advise balsa plugs for conditions of extreme calm, a slightly noisier model for an

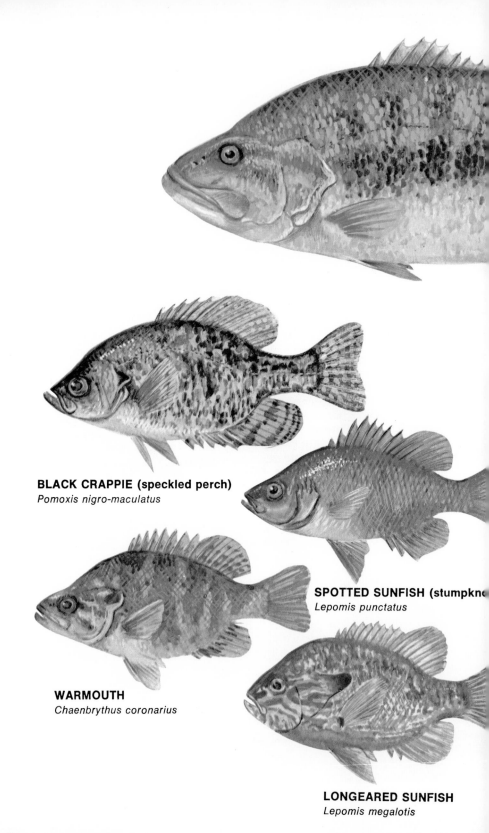

BLACK CRAPPIE (speckled perch)
Pomoxis nigro-maculatus

SPOTTED SUNFISH (stumpkn
Lepomis punctatus

WARMOUTH
Chaenbrythus coronarius

LONGEARED SUNFISH
Lepomis megalotis

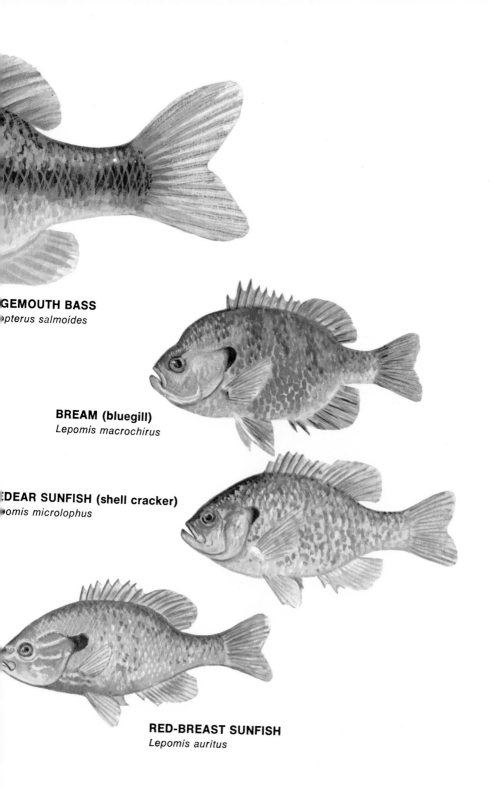

GEMOUTH BASS
pterus salmoides

BREAM (bluegill)
Lepomis macrochirus

DEAR SUNFISH (shell cracker)
omis microlophus

RED-BREAST SUNFISH
Lepomis auritus

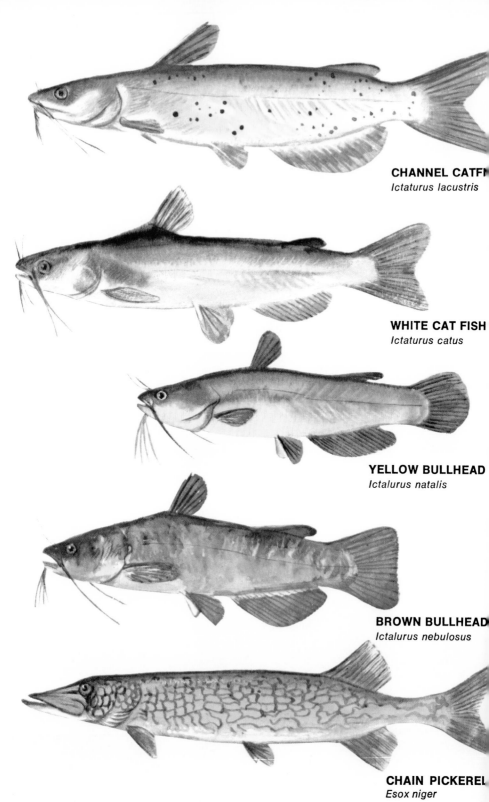

CHANNEL CATFI
Ictaturus lacustris

WHITE CAT FISH
Ictaturus catus

YELLOW BULLHEAD
Ictalurus natalis

BROWN BULLHEAD
Ictalurus nebulosus

CHAIN PICKEREL
Esox niger

average ripple on the water, and a very noisy one that bloops or chugs for rougher water. But these are only guidelines. Sometimes it's necessary to go against the book and do your own experimenting.

When live-baiting for bass, there is no better all-around bait to use than the native golden shiner, or, if those are unavailable, the commercial shiners sold everywhere. Another great bait, overlooked by many folks, is a small bluegill.

Largemouth bass average only one or two pounds in weight — that being the size the species attains in southern waters in only a year or so of growth. But bass scaling four to eight pounds are always at least fairly good prospects in most bass waters. Ten to 15-pounders fall to lucky fishermen throughout Florida, and in some other southern states as well, while rarely an 18 or 19-pounder might find his way to the end of the line. Or I should say "her" way, since all lunker bass are females.

The world record largemouth of 22½ pounds was caught in Georgia in 1932. The largemouth is one of the two most common bass species in the United States, the other, of course, being the smallmouth, which is found only in cooler waters outside Florida.

Another species of sweetwater fish which attracts mass attention is the crappie, commonly called speckled perch or "speck" in many southern areas, including all of Florida. Though crappie can be caught at any time of year they are by far the most plentiful in winter and early spring. The universal bait is a live minnow, usually fished on a cane pole with about a No. 4 or No. 6 hook.

But the crappie is a good casting fish too, especially if you use ultra-light spinning tackle and throw little jigs only an inch or so long. Fly fishermen can do well with little streamers or flyrod spoons. Normally, a sinking fly line should be used, since most specks are nabbed a few feet under the surface. At times, though, I have caught a few on popping bugs.

Then there are the "bream" — a blanket name given throughout the South to all the smaller members of the sunfish family, including bluegill, longear sunfish or shellcracker, pumpkinseed, redbreast, warmouth, stumpknocker and a few others.

They are panfish, all, but great sport and most of them are willing biters on everything from earthworms and a dozen other natural baits to spinning lures and flies. Like everybody else who casts for bass, I often have a bluegill or other bream slug a big casting plug not much smaller than itself, which demonstrates how aggressive the little cusses are.

From my observations, the most-used natural bait, aside from the ever-present worms, are crickets and a variety of caterpillars. Bream are easily chummed with bits of bread, and this makes them even more receptive to either bait or lure.

To fly-fish for bream, try an assortment of lures that includes small popping bugs, sponge-rubber spiders and sinking lures such as the molded mayfly nymph or molded cricket. Small dry flies and streamers are usually effective, too.

Sharks and Rays

Sharks and rays make up a large group of soft-spined fishes which hold great fascination for mankind. Some of them are among the deadliest creatures in the world, and others among the biggest. Many are fine game fish, even though they appeal to only a relatively small percentage of anglers. But one thing is certain. Just about every member of this group is keenly interesting, not only to scientists, but to the general public as well.

As game fish, sharks play many roles. The heaviest catch in sports fishing history was a 2,664-pound great white shark that measured 16 feet, 10 inches. Imagine a one and one-quarter ton game fish on the end of your line — especially one which would gladly catch you if the situation were only in his favor instead of vice versa! And if you can picture that one, then try to picture a white shark more than 30 feet long. Reliable observers have reported them that big. Among other giant sharks that have fallen to anglers were a tiger shark scaling 1780 pounds, and a mako weighing 1061.

Though all three world-record catches were made in the Pacific, those same species do occur in South Atlantic waters, and several tiger sharks exceeding 1000 pounds have been taken on this side of the world.

Of all the "sporting" sharks, the mako seems to be the best liked by big game fishermen. I suppose this is because the mako can make spectacular jumps, and there's no doubt the species

does merit classification as a good game fish. But in my opinion there are some other species which are equally tough, maybe even a bit tougher, though not as showy.

One of the most rugged is the great hammerhead. Now maybe the hammerhead isn't the most common of offshore sharks in tropical and sub-tropical waters, but it is *seen* by big game fishermen more than any other, because of its habit of swimming at the surface with dorsal fin and tail fin out of the water. Hook a big hammerhead and you'll have your hands full. For that matter, almost any big shark is a rough customer on rod and reel — the lemon, the bull, the tiger and numerous others.

I'll admit that small sharks which grab your bait and tie you up while you're fishing for other varieties can be a great nuisance. And I've also been known to say bad things about big sharks that have taken prize fish off the end of my line. But as quite a few shark-fishing specialists already know, there is great sport in going after the saw-toothed monsters. And best of all, you can do it everywhere in salt water, from the shore to the deep sea.

Just as the mako is classed as a prime big-game fish, so do light tackle anglers have glowing praise for another and smaller variety — the blacktip. Along coastal flats and shallows, the blacktip will hit both bait and artificial lures, including surface plugs, and will give you a wild battle that includes some sizzling, twisting jumps. Blacktip sharks also can be found offshore, and their jumping habits there have earned them the name "spinner shark."

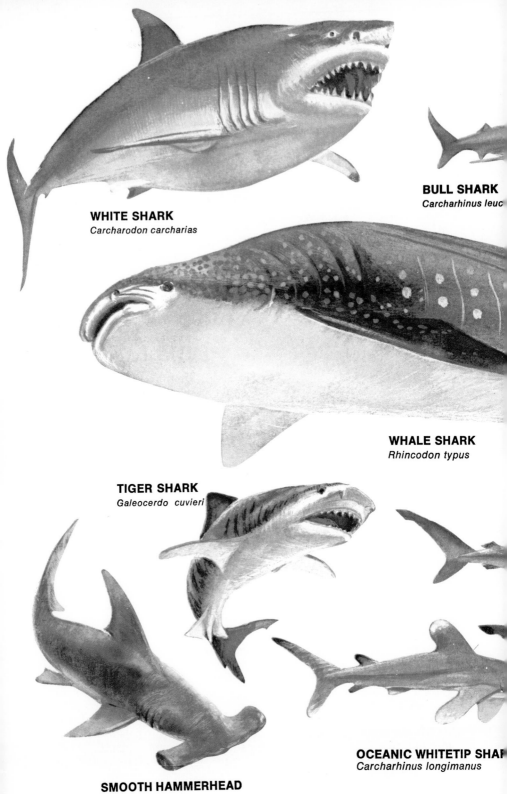

WHITE SHARK
Carcharodon carcharias

BULL SHARK
Carcharhinus leuc

WHALE SHARK
Rhincodon typus

TIGER SHARK
Galeocerdo cuvieri

SMOOTH HAMMERHEAD
Sphyrna zygaena

OCEANIC WHITETIP SHAI
Carcharhinus longimanus

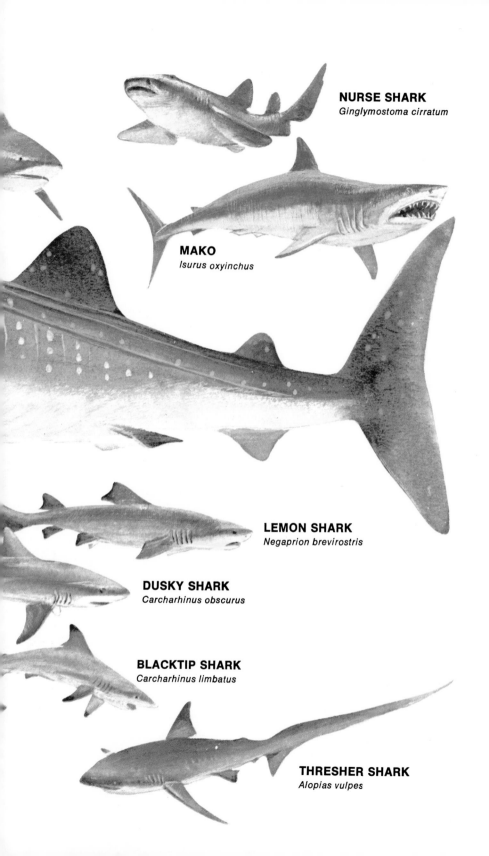

NURSE SHARK
Ginglymostoma cirratum

MAKO
Isurus oxyinchus

LEMON SHARK
Negaprion brevirostris

DUSKY SHARK
Carcharhinus obscurus

BLACKTIP SHARK
Carcharhinus limbatus

THRESHER SHARK
Alopias vulpes

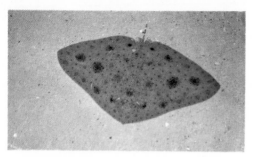

SMOOTH BUTTERFLY RAY
Gymnura micrura

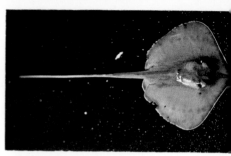

ATLANTIC STINGRAY
Dasyatis sabina

CLEARNOSE SKATE
Raja eglanteria

ELECTRIC RAY
Narcine brasiliensis

SPOTTED EAGLE RAY
Aetobatus narinari

YELLOW STINGRAY
Urolophus jamaicensis

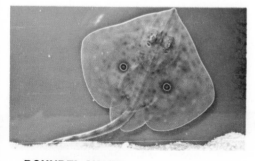

ROUNDEL SKATE
Raja texana

ATLANTIC GUITARFISH
Rhinobatos lentiginosus

A great many anglers are surprised to learn that sharks can be taken on the flyrod with artificial flies — mainly by poling over shallow flats and casting to individual sharks that you spot. This is one of the most absorbing specialties that I know of, and even though I have caught sharks as heavy as 151 pounds on the flyrod in this manner, I still get a big kick out of casting to the little fellows on the flats which might weigh anywhere from five to 50 pounds. In addition to flies, these flats sharks will also hit jigs and plugs, but no matter what kind of artificial lure you throw at them, you must draw it pretty close in front of their noses, because their eyesight is notoriously poor.

Biggest of all sharks is the whale shark, which can grow to 50 feet or more in length and weigh 50,000 pounds or more. Fortunately, this one is not aggressive and, in fact, feeds on extremely tiny organisms in the water, which it collects in great quantity simply by swimming through the sea with its cave-like mouth open.

Almost all other sharks *can* be aggressive, even though the white shark has the widest reputation as a man-eater. Don't trust even the harmless-looking nurse shark. And the angler, of course, must be extremely careful in handling all catches.

The closely-related rays aren't too important to the angler. Only one of them — the sawfish — has ever been listed by the International Game Fish Association. Still, the angler will encounter rays of various sorts whether he likes it or not.

The common sting-rays take bottom baits and put up a pretty darn good tussle. Of course, the outcome is always disappointing because the fisherman has had dreams of some outstanding fish before he gets the flat and ugly apparition in view. Sting rays pose a danger because of the sharp, barbed spikes in their whip-like tails. While experienced fishermen have ways of handling a ray, the newcomer is best advised to cut the line and forget it.

Any fisherman who wades the coastal shallows must keep the threat of sting rays in mind, for here is where the danger is greatest. If you step on one, it will arch the stabbing tail over its back and into your leg. But the precaution while wading is a simple one: just drag your feet along the bottom, rather than picking them up and putting them down. If you touch a ray with a sliding foot, he'll scoot away immediately, with no more harm done than a good scare.

The giant manta is the largest of rays, but despite a story-book name of "devil fish," it is entirely harmless. They entertain more than they alarm by their habit of leaping from the water and re-entering with a booming splash. The graceful leopard ray, which you may see gliding through clear water like an immense butterfly, also leaps freely for your amusement, and also is harmless. The leopard is spike-equipped, but I can't conceive of a situation — other than deliberate handling of this ray — which would allow him a chance to use his daggers on a person.

Common relatives of the rays are skates. They can be troublesome to bottom fishermen but have no weapons with which to cause bodily harm — with one exception. A thankfully rare fellow called the torpedo skate or torpedo ray can effect an electric shock similar to that of the infamous South American electric eel.

Marine Tropicals

I don't know of any hobby more fascinating than collecting and keeping those brilliant living jewels of tropical waters — the little coral-reef fishes.

Now the fact that I've spent the great majority of my off-hours either on top of the water or swimming under it would seem to have no little influence on such an opinion. However, I must point out that my interest is shared nowadays by thousands of people who — unhappily — never get the chance to collect for themselves but who nevertheless are completely intrigued by their salt water aquaria and the entertaining inhabitants thereof.

Are you one of the many folks who *could* collect some of his own fish except for uncertainty, or leeriness, about chasing them in their element? If so, you're missing at least half the fun.

You surely don't need to be a master diver, or a SCUBA expert to collect many lovely types of marine tropicals. With a mask, snorkel, fins and a modest set of collecting equipment you can procure specimens throughout the Florida Keys, or along tropical island shorelines, in water that doesn't necessarily have to be more than five or six feet deep — often only knee-deep.

Isolated coral clumps, or patches, are among the best of hunting grounds anyway, and you'll find many such spots fairly close to shore, or in shoal water a short distance offshore, if you go by boat.

I catch most of my fish, not with a slurp gun (which I find rather ineffective in most instances, and which sometimes can damage the specimens) but with a simple circular net only four feet in diameter.

I ring the outside of the net with lead sinkers, and in the center of it I fix a cork float. In effect, it's like an underwater cast net. But of course you don't cast it, you merely drop it.

You also need what I call a "chase stick" — a metal rod used for poking into holes and chasing the fish out into the net. The chase stick should be of fairly soft metal (even a straightened coat hanger will do a good job) so it can be bent to probe around corners.

Here's how the simple system works. You snorkel at the surface, looking for fish around small patches of coral or heads of large sponges. When you spot a fish you'd like to have, you chase him into a crevice, which is no trouble at all, since the fish stay close to their havens and retreat into them at the least alarm. Then you drop your net over the clump, cutting off all possible escape routes. The last step is to use your chase stick to poke around and send the fish running outside and into the net.

There are numerous other ways to catch specimens underwater, and some collectors do a good job with dip nets. But for all-around effectiveness, and especially if you're inexperienced, the drop net is best of all. You can get the netting material at commercial fishing supply houses. Monofilament is the best material because it is both easy to handle and fast-sinking.

Naturally, you'll need something to keep your fish in when you catch them. This is a simple device, too — a plastic bucket with an inner tube or foam floats around the top to keep it upright and at the surface.

Now when the time comes to set up your salt water aquarium, you should head straight for a reliable dealer and heed his advice. You also should get at least one good book on the subject and learn as much as you can.

You'll need a tank, of course, and the proper filters, and other material to make the habitat both comfortable and liveable for your specimens. Also, you'll want it to have a natural, authentic undersea look.

Now that saltwater aquarium addicts are so widespread and numerous, it's easy to find tanks in a great variety of sizes and shapes. Again, your dealer is the best counselor here. Don't make the mistake of trying to convert a freshwater tank to saltwater use, because the freshwater tanks are usually framed in metal — which corrodes in salt water and can poison your fish.

Size is important as well. If you must have a small tank because of space limitations, the number of fish you can keep will be limited too. You shouldn't try to support more than one fish per gallon of tank capacity.

As far as the water, itself, is concerned, I scoop up my own, preferably from well offshore in the Gulf Stream. The closer to shore you get, the more sediment you're likely to find in the water — and the more pollutants.

Even Gulf Stream water I let stand for at least 24 hours before using, and then I always discard the last gallon of water on the bottom of the container. If you don't have access to good sea water, don't worry. Your pal, the dealer, can fix you up with a saltwater mix that's as easy to make as Kool-Aid. You mix, let stand, and use. But follow directions, of course.

One of the great delights of aquarium keeping is watching and learning the individual characteristics of the different species. Some of the characteristics can lead to unhappy results, so it's important to get the right "mix" of fish in your tank to begin with. Some types are aggressive and bossy, particularly the angel fishes which, being so beautiful, are aquarium favorites.

You shouldn't have much trouble with only one angel. Or you might try two angels of the same species if they are the same size. But you're asking for a lot of headaches if you mingle different sizes of different angelfish species.

Butterfly fish are popular, pretty and calm. But by contrast to the angelfish, are tough to feed.

Any of the demoselles make good additions to an aquarium — beau gregory, marine jewel, sergeant major — and are quite easy to catch and to keep. But they too are aggressive.

Of course, some of your specimens are useful as well as interesting. I'd suggest a pair of neon gobies in the tank because these little fellows keep parasites off the other fish — and they're quite colorful at the same time.

Snails are important because they help keep the tank clean. Small crabs, while interesting to look at, also perform cleaning chores. But don't put a small crawfish (spiny lobster) in your tank, or you might wake up some morning and find all your fish missing. Any fish which is in the least distressed will fall victim to the ravenous lobster. For the same reason, resist any impulse to introduce a sargassum fish into your happy community. This guy — who is easy to find by dipping up bunches of floating sargassum weeds and picking through it — is all mouth and always hungry.

While we're on the subject of sargassum weed, I might point out that you *can* find nice specimens of both fish and crustaceans in the weed if you look through enough of it. But the sargassum fish itself is not one of them.

Your aquarium should be floored with fairly coarse material, such as crushed shell, rather than sand. Your specimens will need some hiding places, and for this, coral is not only good but also an attractive and natural addition to any tank.

If you use living coral, it has to be cleaned. Bleach it thoroughly in a chlorine bleach solution; rinse well and allow to air for 24 hours or more. We're coming to realize that live coral isn't an inexhaustible commodity, so look around for dead coral. This is pretty easy to find. Bleach and treat it like live coral to make sure impurities are removed.

Also, your dealer can provide imitation undersea stuff — not the out-of-place ceramic gadgets you used to see in goldfish bowls, but natural-looking corals and rocks.

Bleached coral may look starkly white when you put it in the tank, but soon will take on subdued, and sometimes quite colorful hues, due to micro-organisms in the water.

If you have access to the seashore you can also find an almost endless variety of shells which make attractive and, in many cases, useful additions to the aquarium by providing more cubbyholes for your specimens. Use these with restraint, however. You don't want to over-clutter your aquarium, so just a minimum assortment of shells in colors and shapes that please you will suffice.

Keeping the water light and temperature well-regulated is very important. I like to change the water in my aquarium completely every three to six months. Other folks change about a fourth of the water every month. Well-positioned lights can increase the dramatic effect and attractiveness of your aquarium, though you should take care that artificial lighting is not used so much that there's a danger of raising the water temperature too high. You don't want the water to get too cold, either. Remember, these are tropical fish and they like things warm. Temperatures should stay about 75° or 80°.

All in all, you do have to put a considerable amount of thought, care and attention into keeping a flourishing saltwater aquarium — much more than for freshwater fish. But that's what a hobby should be: something to work at. And few hobbies can offer you more varied pleasures: from the thrill and exercise of collecting, to the relaxing entertainment of observing your own little underwater kingdom.

Deep Water Fish

What sort of sport and food fish dwell in the ocean depths, far down beyond the reach of ordinary sporting tackle? A great many — and only in fairly recent years has any sort of exploratory fishing begun to give a glimmer of the varieties available.

As a rule, the deepest sport fish for which anglers fish the ocean bottom are warsaw grouper and amberjack — along with some smaller types of grouper and snapper. Fishing is at depths of about 200 to 300 feet; and tilefish to perhaps 500 or 600 feet. Even then, the wire lines and heavy sinkers involved make the endeavor more work than fun — so much so that power attachments often are used on the larger sportsfishing reels.

And for true exploratory bottom fishing at greater depths, even the powered sports reels are far from adequate. People with a scientific or commercial interest in this field use custom-engineered "tackle" featuring gasoline-powered winches for reels, along with a short boom, firmly bolted to deck or gunwale, for a rod. The line is very heavy cable, and strong rubber snubbers are used in conjunction to lessen shock.

Numerous varieties of little-known grouper and snapper are hauled up — delicious eating all. I found years ago that the truly deepwater fish are much more delicious than some of their close relatives caught in shallow water — probably due to the great pressures making their flesh more tender and succulent.

Most people figure that if you get a bait way down to the bottom of the deep ocean, you might tie up with some kind of sea monster — and indeed you might. Experimental fishermen have at times seen their heaviest hooks straightened; their strongest cable snapped. Huge sharks, probably. But nobody ever really knows for sure when it happens. As with food fish, there certainly are unknown and little-known species of shark down there — along with oddball fish that no one but a scientist would recognize.

No, I wouldn't call it gamefishing, but I have made quite a few trips with power-winch gear just to see what might come up. Out of sheer interest in all fish that might swim the seas, I'll make more such trips at every opportunity.

SNAPPER
s vivanus

QUEEN SNAPPER
Etelis oculatus

K SNAPPER
dentatus

LONGTAIL BASS
Hemanthias leptus

KFIN SNAPPER
s buccanella

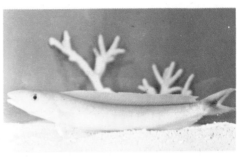

SAND TILEFISH
Malacanthus plumieri

RA SNAPPER
s cyanopterus

TILEFISH
Lopholatilus chamaeleonticeps

YELLOWLINE TILEFISH
Canlolotilus cyanops

YELLOWFIN GROUPER (Young)
Epinephelus venenosa

CONEY (golden hind)
Epinephelus fulvus

WRECKFISH
Polyprion americanus

YELLOWFIN GROUPER
Mycteroperca venenosa

WARSAW GROUPER
Epinephelus nigritus

SNOWY GROUPER
Epinephelus niveatus

OILFISH
Ruvettus pretiosus

70

...NCH ANGELFISH
...canthus paru

BLACKBELLY ROSEFISH
Helicolenus dactylopterus

...E ANGELFISH
...canthus bermudensis

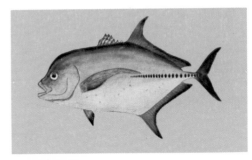

BLACK JACK
Caranx lugubris

...JNG) BLUE ANGELFISH
...anthus bermudensis

BIGEYE
Priacanthus arenatus

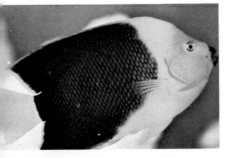

...K BEAUTY
...canthus tricolor

SHORT BIGEYE
Pirshgings alta

(YOUNG) ROCK BEAUTY
Holacanthus tricolor

CHERUBFISH
Centropyge argi

QUEEN ANGELFISH
Holacanthus ciliarus

FOUREYE BUTTERFLYFISH
Chaetodon capistratus

GREY ANGELFISH
arcuatus

SPOTFIN BUTTERFLYFISH
Chaetodon ocellatus

(YOUNG) GREY ANGELFISH
arcuatus

REEF BUTTERFLYFISH
Chaetodon sedentarius

GSNOUT BUTTERFLYFISH
athodes aculeatus

SEA BREAM
Archosargus rhomboidalis

SS PORGY
nus arctifrons

SPOTTAIL PINFISH
Diplodus holbrooki

CEREYE PORGY
us calamus

PINFISH
Lagodon rhomboides

MUDA CHUB
sus sectatrix

COTTONWICK
Haemulon melanurum

73

SPOTTED GOATFISH
Pseudupeneus maculatus

SAILORS CHOICE
Haemulon parrai

YELLOW GOATFISH
Mulloidichthys martinicus

YELLOWFIN MOJARRA
Gerres cinereus

BLUE TANG
Acanthurus coeruleus

ATLANTIC CROAKER
Micropogon undulatus

DOCTORFISH
Acanthurus chirurgus

REEF CROAKER
Odontoscion dentex

GFISH
nolaimus maximus

BEAUGREGORY
Pomacentrus leucostictus

ANISH HOGFISH
ianus rufus

YELLOWTAIL DAMSELFISH
Microspathodon chrysurus

OTFIN HOGFISH
ianus pulchellus

DUSKY DAMSELFISH
Pomacentrus fuscus

YAL GRAMMA
mma loreto

BICOLOR DAMSELFISH
Pomacentrus partitus

YELLOWTAIL REEFFISH
Chromis enchrysurus

CRESTED GOBY
Lophogobius cyprinoides

THREESPOT DAMSELFISH
Pomacentrus planifrons

RUSTY GOBY
Quisquilius hipoliti

BLUE CHROMIS
Chromis cyaneus

SPOTFIN JAWFISH
Opistognathus macrognathus

NEON GOBY
Gobiosoma oceanops

YELLOWHEAD JAWFISH
Opistognathus aurifrons

RRED CARDINALFISH
gon binotatus

BLACKFIN CARDINAL FISH
Astrapogon puncticulatus

AMEFISH
gon maculatus

YELLOWCHEEK WRASSE
Halichoeres cyanocephalus

NCHFISH
apogon stellatus

CLOWN WRASSE
Halichoeres maculipinna

ASSEYE SNAPPER
canthus cruentatus

BLACKEAR WRASSE
Halichoeres poeyi

77

PAINTED WRASSE
Halichoeres caudalis

PUPPINGWIFE (Young)
Halichoeres radiatus

YELLOWHEAD WRASSE
Halichoeres garnoti

SLIPPERY DICK
Halichoeres bivittatus

BLUEHEAD
Thalassoma bifasciatum

MOLLY MILLER
Blennius cristatus

PUDDINGWIFE
Halichoeres radiatus

GREEN RAZORFISH
Hemipteronotus splendens

SH TRIGGERFISH
dermis maculatus

JACKKNIFE-FISH
Equetus lanceolatus

CK DURGON
thys niger

ORANGE SPOTTED FILEFISH
Cautherhines pullus

HAT
s acuminatus

PLANEHEAD FILEFISH
Monacanthus hispidus

TED DRUM
s punctatus

FRINGED FILEFISH
Monacanthus ciliatus

ATLANTIC MOONFISH
Vomer setapinnis

HORSE-EYE JACK
Caranx latus

LOOKDOWN (Young)
Selene vomer

ALMACO JACK
Seriola rivoliana

LEATHERJACKET
Oligoplites saurus

BLUNT NOSE JACK
Hemicaraux amblyrhynchus

PERMIT (Young)
Trachinotus falcatus

RAINBOW RUNNER
Elagatis bipinnulata

RY BLENNY
omus nuchipinnis

REEF SQUIRRELFISH
Holocentrus coruscus

FIN BLENNY
naria pandionis

DUSKY SQUIRRELFISH
Holocentrus vexillarius

P BLENNY
ennius atlanticus

BLACKBAR SOLDIERFISH
Myripristis jacobus

DA BLENNY
les saburrae

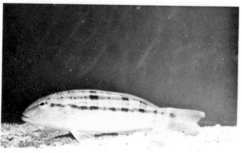

SAND PERCH
Diplectrum formosum

SOUTHERN KINGFISH
Menticirrhus americanus

YELLOWMOUTH GROUPER
Mycteroperca interstitialis

CREOLE-FISH
Paranthias furcifer

CONEY
Epinephelus fulva

MARBLED GROUPER
Dermatolepis inermis

RED HIND
Epinephelus guttatus

RED GROUPER
Epinephelus morio

BLACK HAMLET
Hypoplectrus nigricans

RRED HAMLET
oplectrus puella

BLUE HAMLET
Hypoplectrus gemma

TTON HAMLET
estes afer

BLACK SEA BASS
Centropristis striata

LOW BELLY HAMLET
oplectrus aberrans

BANK SEA BASS
Centropristis ocyurus

GO HAMLET
plectrus indigo

LANTERN BASS
Serranus baldwini

CHALK BASS
Serranus tortugarum

BELTED SANDFISH
Serranus subligarius

HARLEQUIN BASS
Serranus tigrinus

REDSPOTTED HAWKFISH
Amblycirrhitus pinos

TOBACCOFISH
Serranus tabacarius

GAFFTOPSAIL CATFISH
Bagre marinus

GREATER SOAPFISH
Rypticus soponaceus

CATFISH
Arius felis

TRIPED PARROTFISH
arus croicensis

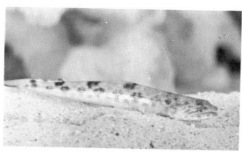

INSHORE LIZARDFISH
Synodus foetens

UELIP PARROTFISH
ptotomus roseus

ATLANTIC MIDSHIPMAN
Porichthys plectrodon

NBOW PARROTFISH
us quacamaia

ATLANTIC FLYINGFISH
Cypselurus heterurus

KEFISH
hinocephalus myops

PEACOCK FLOUNDER
Bothus lunatus

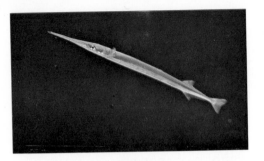

ATLANTIC NEEDLEFISH
Strogylura marina

HARVESTFISH
Perpilus alepidotus

ATLANTIC THREAD HERRING
Opisthonema oglinum

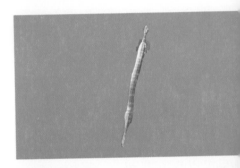

TRUMPETFISH
Aulostomus maculatus

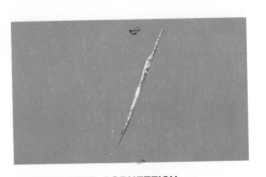

BLUESPOTTED CORNETFISH
Fistularia tabacaria

SOUTHERN PUFFER
Sphoeroides hephelus

SPOTTED TRUNKFISH
Lactophrys trigonis

BANDTAILED PUFFER
Sphoeroides spengleri

NOSE PUFFER
ster rostrata

SARGASSUMFISH
Histrio histrio

-DOT BATFISH
halus radiatus

MAN-OF-WAR FISH
Nomeus gronovii

ED BURRFISH
cterus schoepfi

BLACK DRIFTFISH
Hyperoplyphe bythites

URRFISH
cterus antillarum

REMORA
Remora remora

SHARKSUCKER
Echeneis naucrates

SKILLETFISH
Gobiesox strumosus

SOUTHERN SENNET
Sphyraena picudilla

SPOTTED SEAHORSE
Hippocampus erectus

SPOTTED DRIFTFISH
Ariomma regulus

DWARF SEAHORSE
Hippocampus zosterae

BARRELFISH
Hyperoglyphe perciformis

LONGSNOUT SEAHORSE (Young)
Hippocampus reidi

NGSNOUT SEAHORSE
pocampus reidi

SPLITLURE FROGFISH
Antennarius scaber

CEAN SUNFISH
la mola

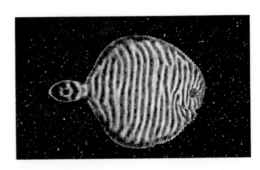

NAKED SOLE
Gymnachirus melas

ULF TOADFISH
sanus beta

BARBFISH
Scorpoena brasiliensi

CELLATED FROGFISH
tennarius ocellatus

REEF SCORPIONFISH
Scorpaenodes caribbaeus

MUSHROOM SCORPIONFISH
Scorpaena inermis

GREEN MORAY
Gymnothorax funebris

BIGHEAD SEAROBIN
Prionotus tribulus

SPOTTED MORAY
Gymnothorax moringa

SOUTHERN STARGAZER
Astroscopus y-graecum

PURPLEMOUTH MORAY
Gymnothorax vicinus

FLYING GURNARD
Dactylopterus volitans

BLACKEDGE MORAY
Gymnothorax nigromarginatus

ER MORAY
elycore nigricans

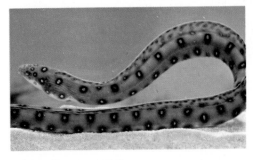

GOLDSPOTTED EEL
Myrichthys oculatus

IN MORAY
Ina catenata

SHRIMP EEL
Ophichthus gomesi

DENTAIL MORAY
ena miliaris

SMALLTOOTH SAWFISH
Pristis pectinata

RPTAIL EEL
hthys acuminatus

ATLANTIC STURGEON
Acipeuser oxyrhychus

91

Cross Index

Albacore 17
Amberjack, Greater 32
Angelfish, Blue 71
Angelfish, Blue (young) 71
Angelfish, French 34, 71
Angelfish, Gray 34, 72
Angelfish, Queen 34, 72

Barbfish 89
Barracuda, Great 32
Barrelfish 88
Bass, Bank Sea 83
Bass, Black Sea 83
Bass, Harlequin 84
Bass, Lantern 83
Bass, Largemouth 54
Beaugregory 75
Bigeye 71
Bigeye, Short 71
Blenny, Florida 81
Blenny, Hairy 81
Blenny, Redlip 81
Blenny, Sailfin 81
Bluefish 27
Bluehead 78
Bonefish 46
Bonito, Oceanic 16
Bream 55
Bream, Sea 73
Bullhead, Brown 56
Bullhead, Yellow 56
Burrfish, Striped 87
Burrfish, Web 87
Butterflyfish, Banded 34
Butterflyfish, Foureye 34, 72
Butterflyfish, Longsnout . . 34, 73
Butterflyfish, Reef 72
Butterflyfish, Spotfin 72

Cardinalfish, Barred 77
Cardinalfish, Blackfin 77
Catfish 56, 84
Catfish, Channel 56
Catfish, Gafftopsail 84
Catfish, White 56
Chalkfish 84
Cherubfish 72
Chromis, Blue 76
Chub, Bermuda 27, 73
Cobia 45
Conchfish 77
Coney 82

Coney (Golden Hind) 70
Coney, Golden 29
Cornetfish, Bluespotted 86
Cowfish 26
Crappie, Black 54
Creole Fish 82
Croaker, Atlantic 74
Croaker, Reef 74

Damselfish, Bicolor 75
Damselfish, Dusky 75
Damselfish, Threespot 76
Damselfish, Yellowtail 75
Doctorfish 27, 74
Dolphin 11
Driftfish, Spotted 88
Drum 45
Drum, Red 45
Drum, Spotted 79
Durgon, Black 79

Eel, Goldspotted 91
Eel, Sharptail 91
Eel, Shrimp 91

Filefish, Fringed 79
Filefish, Orange 26
Filefish, Orangespotted 79
Filefish, Planehead 79
Filefish, Scrawled 26
Flamefish 77
Flounder, Broad 45
Flounder, Peacock 85
Flying Fish, Atlantic 17, 85
Frogfish, Occelated 89
Frogfish, Splitture 89

Gag 28
Goatfish, Spotted 74
Goatfish, Yellow 74
Goby, Crested 76
Goby, Neon 76
Goby, Rusty 76
Graysby 30
Grouper, Black 30
Grouper, Marbled 30, 82
Grouper, Nassau 30
Grouper, Red 82
Grouper, Sickle-fin 28
Grouper, Snowy 70
Grouper, Tiger 30
Grouper, Warsaw 28, 70
Grouper, Yellowfin 70

Grouper, Yellowfin (young) . . 70
Grouper, Yellowmouth 82
Grunt, Bluestriped 26
Grunt, French 26
Grunt, Spanish 26
Guitarfish, Atlantic 62
Gurnard, Flying 90

Hamlet, Barred 83
Hamlet, Black 82
Hamlet, Blue 83
Hamlet, Indigo 83
Hamlet, Mutton 25
Hamlet, Yellowbelly 83
Harvestfish 86
Hawkfish 84
High Ha 79
Hind, Red 30
Hind, Rock 30
Hogfish 75
Hogfish, Spotfin 75

Jack, Almaco 80
Jack, Bar 32
Jack, Black 71
Jack, Bluntnose 80
Jack, Crevalle 32
Jack, Horse-eye 80
Jackknife Fish 79
Jawfish, Spotfin 76
Jewfish, Yellowhead 76
Jewfish 28

Kingfish, Southern 82

Ladyfish 46
Leatherjacket 80
Lizardfish, Inshore 85
Lookdown 33
Lookdown (young) 80
Loreto, Gramma 75

Mackerel, Cero 10
Mackerel, King 10
Mackerel, Spanish 10
Man-of-War Fish 87
Margate 26
Margate, Black 26
Marlin, Blue 14
Marlin, White 14
Midshipman, Atlantic 85
Mojarra 74
Molly Miller 78
Moonfish, Atlantic 80

Moray, Blackedge 90
Moray, Chain 91
Moray, Goldentail 91
Moray, Green 90
Moray, Purplemouth 90
Moray, Spotted 90
Moray, Vipor 91
Mullet, Fantail 46

Needlefish, Atlantic 86

Oilfish 70

Palometa 33
Parrotfish, Blue 35
Parrotfish, Blue Tip 85
Parrotfish, Green 35
Parrotfish, Midnight 35
Parrotfish, Rainbow 35, 85
Parrotfish, Spotfin 35
Parrotfish, Stoplight 35
Parrotfish, Striped 85
Permit 32
Permit (young) 80
Pickerel 56
Pinfish 73
Pinfish, Spottail 73
Polka-dot Batfish 87
Pompano, African 32
Pompano, Florida 32
Porgy, Grass 73
Porgy (Saucereye) 26, 73
Porkfish 27
Puddingwife 78
Puddingwife (young) 78
Puffer, Bandtailed 86
Puffer, Checkered 86
Puffer, Sharpnose 87

Ray, Electric 62
Ray, Smooth Butterfly 62
Ray, Spotted Eagle 62
Razorfish, Green 78
Reeffish, Yellowtail 76
Remora 87
Rock Beauty 34, 71
Rock Beauty (young) 72
Rosefish, Blackbelly 71
Rudderfish 87
Runner, Blue 32
Runner, Rainbow 80

Sailfish 7
Sailfish, Atlantic 14

Sailor's Choice 74
Sandfish, Belted 84
Sand Perch 81
Sargassumfish 87
Sawfish, Smalltooth 91
Scorpionfish, Mushroom 90
Scorpionfish, Reef 89
Seahorse, Dwarf 88
Seahorse, Longsnout 89
Seahorse, Longsnout (young) 88
Seahorse, Spotted 88
Searobin, Bighead 90
Seatrout, Spotted 45
Sennet, Southern 88
Sergeant Major 27
Shark, Black Tip 61
Shark, Bull 60
Shark, Dusky Ground 61
Shark, Hammerhead 60
Shark, Lemon 61
Shark, Mako 61
Shark, Nurse 61
Shark, Oceanic Whitetip 60
Shark, Thresher 61
Shark, Tiger 60
Shark, Whale 60
Shark, White 60
Sharksucker 88
Sheepshead 46
Skate, Clearnose 62
Skate, Roundel 62
Skilletfish 88
Slippery Dick 78
Snakefish 85
Snapper, Black 69
Snapper, Blackfin 69
Snapper, Cardinal 69
Snapper, Cubera 69
Snapper, Dog 24
Snapper, Glasseye 77
Snapper, Grey 24
Snapper, Lane 24
Snapper, Mutton 25
Snapper, Queen 69
Snapper, Red 24
Snapper, Schoolmaster 24
Snapper, Silk 69
Snapper, Yellowtail 25
Snook 39, 44
Soapfish 84
Soldierfish, Blackbar 81

Sole, Naked 89
Spadefish, Atlantic 27
Spearfish, Longbill 15
Squirrelfish 26
Squirrelfish, Dusky 81
Squirrelfish, Reef 81
Stargazer, Southern 90
Stingray, Atlantic 62
Stingray, Yellow 62
Sturgeon, Atlantic 91
Sunfish 54, 55
Sunfish, Longeared 54
Sunfish, Ocean 89
Sunfish, Red-Breast 55
Sunfish, Readear 55
Sunfish, Spotted 54
Swordfish 15

Tang, Blue 74
Tarpon 43, 46
Thread Herring, Atlantic 86
Tilefish 30
Tilefish, Blue 69
Tilefish, Sand 69
Tilefish, Yellowline 70
Toadfish, Gulf 89
Tobaccofish 84
Triggerfish, Black 27
Triggerfish, Gray 27
Triggerfish, Ocean (tally) 27
Triggerfish, Rough 79
Triggerfish, Queen 27
Triggerfish, Queen (tally) 27
Tripletail 46
Trumpetfish 86
Trunkfish 27
Trunkfish, Spotted 86
Tuna, Blackfin 17
Tuna, Bluefin 16
Tuna, Little 16
Tuna, Yellowfin 17

Wahoo 10
Warmouth 54
Wrasse, Black Ear 77
Wrasse, Clown 77
Wrasse, (Hogfish) 25
Wrasse, Painted 78
Wrasse, Spanish Hogfish . 25, 75
Wrasse, Yellowcheek 77
Wrasse, Yellowhead 78
Wreckfish 70

LIMITED EDITION, FULL COLOR PRINT

"101 FISH OF THE SOUTH ATLANTIC"

This is a small reproduction of the complete fish painting by Russ Smiley. The fish are shown full size to illustrate this book.

You can own this large (24" x 34") limited edition art print, signed by Russ Smiley. This full color lithograph on heavy, luxurious paper stock is ideal for framing for home or office. It also makes a perfect gift for the fisherman. To receive this print of 101 fish of the south Atlantic, send $40.00 plus $5.00 for postage and handling along with your name and address to Russ Smiley, 8501 N.E. 4th Ave. Road, Miami, FL 33138. Florida residents add 5% sales tax. If you are not delighted simply return for full refund.

Russ Smiley has been drawing fish for 40 years — his art has appeared in National Geographic, Sports Afield, Fin etc. He illustrated the "Guide to the Everglades National Park and Florida Keys". His original paintings, of fish, wildlife and landscapes hang in many private collections. Russ's illustrations and pictorial maps and limited edition prints have received National recognition.

Many thanks to Mr. Burton Clark and the Miami Seaquarium for their help and reproduction rights to their very valuable 35 MM fish film file which has taken over twenty years to compile. Thanks also to Dr. C. Richard Robins and Vic Dunaway, who checked fish facts etc. We also greatly appreciate the loan of (marlin, snook, bass) paintings from Mr. Joe Muxo's private collection.